AI Prompts For Absolute Beginners Over Fifty

The Prompt Recipe Method - Simple Templates & Calm Somatic Habits for Better AI Responses Across Multiple Platforms

Margaret Fields

1957 Publishing

This Book Belongs To:

AI Prompts for Absolute Beginners Over Fifty: The Prompt Recipe Method - Simple Templates & Calm Somatic Habits for Better AI Responses Across Multiple Platforms

Cover Design by: Margaret Fields

ISBN: 978-1-923524-37-8 (Paperback)

ISBN: 978-1-923524-38-5 (Hard Cover)

About the author

Margaret Fields is a career industrialist, researcher, and independent author who has spent a lifetime mastering the intersection of traditional manual craftsmanship and advanced technology. With a professional background in operational leadership, heavy machinery, and material extraction - including pioneering industrial automation by importing her region's very first stone-milling robot - she brings a uniquely grounded, human perspective to the digital world.

Holding a Master of Arts degree and graduating as Dux of her business college, Margaret values high-utility, actionable problem-solving. Yet, her heart remains firmly rooted in the peace and quiet of her 200-acre rural farm. When she isn't writing or consulting, she is actively planting her seasonal orchard, practicing heritage culinary skills like sourdough baking and tallow production, sculpting, or ballroom dancing.

As a mother and grandmother, Margaret writes the Digital Daisies & Curious Bytes series with a single, clear mission: to dismantle cold corporate jargon and replace it with warm, pressure-free frameworks that respect the intelligence and rich life experience of mature creators. Writing from her kitchen table, she views artificial intelligence not as a complex programming puzzle but as a respectful, highly efficient assistant built to serve her everyday life. Margaret is dedicated to helping readers navigate the modern industrial landscape entirely on their own terms - one beautiful, stress-free prompt at a time.

Dedication

For the quiet searchers

For those who wait until the house is still, this page is for you.

Pull your chair close to our table, wrap your hands around a warm mug, and let out the long, slow breath you have been holding for far too many seasons. This book belongs entirely to you.

It is dedicated to the remarkably brave beginners over fifty who have looked across the modern digital landscape, felt that familiar flutter of hesitation, and chosen to step forward anyway. To those who have opened an AI tool, stared at the empty prompt box, and felt that beautiful mixture of curiosity, hope, and determination.

The modern world moves at a dizzying pace. Advertisements, news headlines, and technology companies often speak in a language that makes it seem as though everyone else received a handbook for the digital age while yours somehow got lost in the mail. It is easy to feel behind. Easy to believe there is a secret code that everyone else understands.

But technology is merely a tool. A machine built to follow instructions. And instructions require context, judgment, life experience, and common sense – the exact qualities you have spent decades developing.

This dedication is for the silent hours nobody else saw. The afternoons when the front door clicked shut, the house grew quiet, and you sat in your favorite chair trying to figure this all out on your own terms. I know those hours well. I know the frustration of clicking through endless technical articles, dodging advertisements, and searching for a simple answer written in plain English rather than a manual designed to impress software experts.

You were never failing in those quiet moments. You were simply being handed instructions written for a computer chip rather than a human being.

This book is also dedicated, with affection and respect, to everyone who has ever swallowed their pride and asked a younger relative, friend, or coworker for help.

We have all stood there while someone closes three windows, opens four apps, changes a dozen settings, and cheerfully announces, "There, see? It's easy!" Meanwhile, we are left standing on the kitchen tiles feeling more confused than when we first asked the question.

The irony is that the very generation that helped build the modern world is so often made to feel small by a blinking cursor or a flat desktop screen. Yet you have already navigated extraordinary technological change. You moved from ledger books to calculators, from paper maps to GPS, from bank tellers to self-service screens. Every time, you adapted because you understood the purpose behind the tool.

Your gray hair is not a limitation. It is an advantage.

The younger generation may move more quickly through menus and settings, but you possess something far more valuable: context. You know what a thoughtful letter should say. You can spot a mistake from a mile away. You understand people, priorities, families, communities, and real-world consequences.

The machine holds the digital pencil, but your life experience is what guides the hand.

And that is why this book was written for you.

So, to the beginners who refused to let the blinking cursor look like a dare: thank you. Thank you for your patience, quiet resilience, and willingness to step outside your comfort zone to claim your rightful place in the modern industrial landscape.

You no longer need to hide your learning in an empty house. You do not need to apologize for moving at your own magnificent, dignified pace, and you never have to feel embarrassed for demanding a technical guide that treats you like an intellectual equal. We are flipping the script completely. We are leaving the complex engineering behind and focusing entirely on what brings ease, organization, and creative joy back into your hands.

This toolkit is your protective safety net. It is your invitation to sit at our digital kitchen table with absolute peace of mind, knowing that you cannot break the system, you cannot press a wrong button that cannot be instantly fixed, and you are entirely capable of mastering this asset on your own terms. Your digital confidence is not a distant dream; it is an active reality that begins the moment you turn the page.

The table is clear, the coffee is warm, and the gate is wide open. This book is written for you, inspired by you, and dedicated to your continued, independent success.

Epigraph

Notes from Margaret's Kitchen Table

"Do not let the speed of the modern landscape deceive you. The most powerful engine on earth remains a clear human mind, speaking plain words, directed by decades of common sense. The machine holds the pen, but you are always the author."

- Margaret Fields

Contents

Introduction

Why My Nephew Became a Prawn

Let me tell you about the time I trusted spellcheck more than my own two eyes.

It was a last-minute birthday card - printed in a hurry, of course - with a sweet little personalized poem inside. I'd checked the layout, admired the font, and hit print, feeling rather pleased with myself. Technology had helped. Job done.

Except it hadn't.

Spellcheck, in its quiet confidence, had decided the recipient's name was wrong. Very wrong. And without asking, it corrected it to Prawn.

Every single reference.

My nephew and I noticed at exactly the same time - that awful split second where your brain says, No... surely not.

I managed to rescue the card just before it was handed over, heart racing, trying not to laugh while also wondering how on earth a computer could look at a perfectly good name and decide:

"No, no. This person is clearly a seafood item."

It was funny... Mortifying... And oddly familiar... Because that's the thing about technology.

It's not malicious... It's not stupid... But it is often incredibly confident.

And if you let it take the lead without understanding how to guide it, you can end up with results that are... well... a little crustacean-adjacent.

Fast forward to today, and we're no longer dealing with spellcheck on birthday cards. We're dealing with powerful AI tools like ChatGPT, Gemini, and Copilot. They're faster. They're smarter. They're more capable. But they still have one thing in common with that spellchecker from all those years ago. They don't know what you meant. They only know what you asked. And that, dear reader, is where this entire book begins.

If you've ever opened an AI tool, stared at the blank box on the screen, and thought: What am I supposed to type? Is there a right way to ask? How do people get these amazing results? Then you are exactly where you need to be.

You are not behind. You are not bad with technology. You are simply standing where millions of people find themselves every day - facing a blinking cursor and wondering what comes next.

The good news? You don't need to learn computer programming. You don't need technical jargon. You don't need to memorize complicated commands. You simply need a better recipe.

And so, that, my friend, is what this book is going to give you.

Welcome to the Prompt Recipe Method.

The Blinking Cursor Problem Picture this:

You settle into your favorite chair, device in hand, and open one of those modern AI chat tools you've been hearing about - perhaps ChatGPT, Gemini, or Copilot.

The screen is clean, bright, and mostly empty. And there it is. A small blank box. Inside it, a single cursor blinks.

Blink... Blink. ..Blink.

It feels a little like a silent dare, doesn't it? Maybe you opened the tool with a clear goal in mind. Perhaps you wanted to draft a thoughtful email, gather fresh dinner ideas, or plan a weekend trip.

Then the questions arrive:

What am I supposed to type? Is there a right way to ask? Am I going to get a useless answer?

Suddenly, a simple task feels harder than it should. The cursor keeps blinking, and before long, you may find yourself closing the tab and deciding to do things the old way instead.

Part of the problem is that most of us learned to use search engines first. We type a few keywords and receive a long list of links, advertisements, and websites to sort through ourselves.

AI works differently. The blank space isn't waiting for keywords. It's waiting for a conversation.

Because nobody explained that shift, the blinking cursor often makes a powerful tool feel like a test you never studied for. If this sounds familiar, take comfort in knowing you're in excellent company.

Millions of capable adults find themselves in this exact position every day. The problem isn't your ability. The problem is that most people are taught backward.

The Backward Teaching Trap

Traditional technology guides tend to show buttons before purpose, features before benefits, and instructions before understanding. They teach you what to click before explaining why you would want to use the tool. That creates an immediate mental wall.

Trying to memorize commands without understanding the goal is like assembling a grandfather clock in the dark without ever seeing the finished piece. We're going to flip that approach completely.

Instead of focusing on technical mechanics, we're going to focus on what you want to accomplish in everyday life and use your existing

The Adult Advantage

Think about everything you already know. You have spent decades solving real-world problems, managing households, raising families, building careers, supporting communities, and adapting to change. You possess something incredibly valuable: Context. You know how a thoughtful letter should sound. You understand how a family gathering comes together. You can spot questionable advice from a mile away.

These conversational AI tools work best when paired with exactly that kind of practical wisdom. Your experience isn't a disadvantage. It's an asset.

You have already adapted to enormous technological shifts. You moved from rotary phones to push-button phones, from paper maps to GPS, and from card catalogs to computer screens. You adapted. Then you thrived.

This shift is no different. Yet AI can still make confident, capable people feel uncertain. You may worry that you're "not techy" enough, or feel overwhelmed by unfamiliar language and fast-moving technology. Perhaps you've even asked a younger relative for help.

There is nothing quite like asking a well-meaning grandchild a simple question, only to watch their fingers fly across the screen, closing windows and opening apps before announcing: "There, see? It's easy!"

Meanwhile, you're standing there more confused than when you started. Your younger relative's speed comes from familiarity, not necessarily a deeper understanding. They are comfortable experimenting. You simply haven't been given the chance to learn the tool's underlying rhythm.

Technology isn't a young person's magic trick. It's a tool. And tools can be learned.

Let's clear the air right now: Your intelligence is not the problem. The problem is that most technology books are written by software experts trying to impress other software experts. I didn't write this book to show off technical jargon or build complex systems.

My name is Margaret Fields, and I have spent my career helping adults learn technology without pressure, rushing, or condescension. I believe in clear, practical steps that respect your intelligence, your experience, and your time. I view AI through a completely human lens.

These tools are not digital wizards. They are not reserved for twenty-something software developers. They are simply tools that respond to instructions - and learning how to give those instructions is exactly what we're going to do together.

Café note: What AI really is

Imagine AI not as a frightening, cold super-computer, but simply as a remarkably helpful, friendly librarian sitting at a vast desk.

This librarian has read millions of books, recipes, histories, and letters. They are sitting there, pencil in hand, completely ready to assist you. They don't have feelings, they don't get impatient, and they will never judge you for asking the same question five different ways. They do not hold opinions, they never get their feelings hurt, and they will happily rewrite a draft fifty times until it sounds exactly the way you want it to. They are just waiting for you to tell them exactly what you need.

The Digital Daisies & Curious Bytes promise

This book is built upon a single, beautiful promise: You will learn a single, easy-to-remember framework that works beautifully across today's most popular AI tools.

There is absolutely no coding required!

You do not need a computer science degree, and you will never be asked to memorize lines of complex computer programming.

Instead, we are going to look at how to use your existing human language - just plain, everyday English - to get the exact results you want on the very first try.

Here is what makes this book entirely different from the dense manuals lining bookstore shelves:

The text flows naturally across five distinct pillars:

A unified glossary: Every single foundational term - like prompt, output, token, hallucination, or context window - is defined exactly once, in one clear, easy-to-find section at the back of the book.

We will never scatter confusing technical definitions throughout our chapters. If you see an unfamiliar word in a later page, you can comfortably ignore it, knowing its single plain-English explanation is safely waiting for you in the back index.

A single framework: We will use a single core structure called the Prompt Recipe. You will learn it once, master its simple ingredients, and then apply it to everything you do.

Whether you are formatting a checklist, writing a letter, or planning a trip, the core structure remains the same. No need to constantly relearn the wheels of technology.

Platform-neutral lessons: We won't clutter your mind by constantly jumping between apps. The basic principles of clear communication work exactly the same way whether you are using ChatGPT, Gemini, or Copilot.

Platform differences are cleanly tucked into their own single comparison chapter. Elsewhere, the lessons are universal.

Zero overlap or filler: Each chapter focuses on exactly one distinct, practical skill or use-case. One chapter covers writing, another covers organizing, and another covers creative brainstorming. No repeated concepts, and no wasted pages. We treat your reading time with the utmost respect.

Centralized troubleshooting: If something goes slightly sideways, you don't have to hunt through the entire text to find a fix.

All troubleshooting lives in one standalone, easy-to-use chapter. Think of it as a calm roadside assistance guide that you can open whenever the tool gives you an unexpected response.

The unifying anchor: Our somatic resets

There is one more unique element to this book that I am incredibly proud to share with you. This is the heart of our Digital Daisies philosophy.

We live in a world that moves far too fast, and staring at digital screens for hours on end can leave us feeling physically tense, mentally exhausted, and disconnected from our physical surroundings. Have you ever noticed that when you are trying to figure out a tricky piece of technology, your shoulders creep up toward your ears? Have you noticed that you tend to take shallow breaths, or that your eyes begin to feel dry and scratchy?

That is called cognitive fatigue, and it is the absolute enemy of learning.

When your body enters that subtle state of stress, your brain switches into a defensive mode. Your working memory shrinks, your patience thins, and it becomes nearly impossible to retain new information. You are not struggling because the concept is too difficult; you are struggling because your nervous system is tired.

The good news is that we are going to handle this completely differently.

Every single chapter in this book pairs a practical technical lesson with a brief, 5-minute somatic micro-habit designed to calm your nervous system and regulate your brain.

We are going to merge the digital and physical worlds. Think of these somatic resets as small, gentle circuit-breakers for your mind.

Before you dive into a new technical task, or right after you achieve a digital win, I will invite you to step away from the keyboard for just two minutes to stretch, take a deep breath, or reset your eyes.

By taking care of your physical well-being, you will find that tech anxiety completely dissolves.

You will approach the computer with a sense of calm, rooted independence. Learning becomes what it always should have been: a pleasure, not a chore.

How to journey through this book

You do not need to read this book from cover to cover before you start seeing real-world benefits. In fact, I prefer that you don't. Each chapter is designed to stand completely on its own two feet.

If you want to skip straight to the section on writing polite emails to clear out your inbox, go right ahead. If you are actively planning a family gathering and want fresh brainstorming ideas, feel free to jump directly to that page. You are the supervisor of this journey, and you should make this book serve your immediate needs first.

To support you as you explore, I have included a wonderful collection of visual aids, downloadable prompt organizers, and quick-reference guides that you can print out or keep on your device. You will also find recurring structural anchors throughout our journey together:

Café notes: Small, warm pieces of wisdom to keep your perspective grounded and remind you of the big picture.

Sticky notes to self: Quick, practical reminders of things you can safely forget so you don't clutter your mind with unnecessary digital details.

Reader reviver brain breaks: Our signature somatic exercises to keep your body feeling relaxed and your mind completely sharp.

Imagine what becomes possible

Imagine what your daily routine will look like just a few weeks from now. Before long, you will wonder why you used to spend twenty minutes staring at a blank screen trying to find the perfect words for a sensitive note, when your new digital partner can help you find them in ten seconds flat.

You will have a beautifully organized repository of your favorite household recipes, customized packing lists for every season, and clear, summarized outlines of lengthy news articles - all created by you, using your own voice and your own rules. You will be able to hand your assistant a multi-page community proposal or a dense insurance policy update and receive a clear, three-paragraph summary in plain language before your coffee even finishes brewing.

This journey is not about transforming you into a software programmer or a computer wizard. It is simply about giving you the keys to an incredibly efficient, respectful assistant that can make your daily life just a little bit easier, more organized, and deeply creative.

Mistakes along the way are not failures; they are simply the pleasant steps of discovering something new. You cannot break the system, you cannot cause an error that can't be instantly fixed, and you are entirely capable of mastering this tool at your own magnificent pace. There is no deadline here, no supervisor looking over your shoulder, and no grade to be given.

The table is set, the coffee is warm, and the gate is wide open. You don't need to wait until the final page to find your confidence. Let's take our very first step together right now. Turn the page to Chapter 1, and let's secure your very first practical success in under ten minutes.

I am so incredibly glad to be walking this path with you.

Mini-milestone: Preparing your workspace

Before we dive into Chapter 1, let's set a beautiful, intentional path for your reading experience. Find a notebook or open a simple digital note on your phone, and take just sixty seconds to answer these two gentle questions:

What is one everyday task (like writing notes, planning meals, or researching a hobby) that I would love to make easier using AI?

How do I want to feel when I sit down at my device today?

Whenever you feel a hint of digital hesitation creeping back in, return to this page, take a deep breath, and remember that you are entirely in control. Let's begin.

Getting Comfortable and Your First Success

Take a long, slow sip of your coffee. If you are reading this while sitting at a desk, a kitchen table, or relaxing in your favorite armchair, just take a moment to look around the room. Feel the solid weight of the book in your hands or the familiar texture of your device. You are completely safe, you are in total control, and there is absolutely nothing on the line here.

Have you ever stood in a grocery store aisle, your handwritten shopping list crumpled in your hand, wishing someone could just step in and tell you exactly what to cook with the items in your cart? Or perhaps you have sat at your computer, deeply curious about these new digital tools you keep hearing about, only to freeze the moment your eyes hit that empty prompt box.

If so, I want you to take a deep, comforting breath. You are not alone, and you have absolutely nothing to apologize for.

A very dear friend of mine, a retired nurse who spent over thirty years navigating intense, high-stakes hospital environments, once leaned across my kitchen table and quietly admitted something to me. She said she felt more nervous typing her very first question into an AI chat tool than she ever did learning to operate a complex, life-saving piece of medical machinery.

When we broke it down over tea, we realized why: the medical machine came with a clear, respectful manual written for her intelligence. The AI tool, on the other hand, just sat there, giving off a blank stare. The medical machine had physical dials, buttons, and visual gauges that told her exactly what state it was in. The AI screen gave her no clues, no structural boundaries, and no indication of how to begin.

The real issue here has never been you. The issue is simply that these modern tools haven't been introduced in a way that aligns with how we actually use technology in our everyday lives.

Think of it this way: if you have raised children, managed busy households, built careers, run small businesses, volunteered your time for community groups, or mastered the dozens of gadget upgrades that have rolled out over the last few decades, you are already deeply equipped for this journey. This book isn't for computer programmers or digital natives who grew up with a smartphone glued to their palms - it is written specifically for you.

We are looking for practical, stress-free ways to use new tools to save you time, give you wonderful ideas, and perhaps inject a bit of fun into your routine - all without requiring a technical degree. If you know how to send a basic email or use a standard search engine, you already possess every single skill required to become completely independent with AI. You already know how to ask a question, clarify a detail, and evaluate whether an answer makes practical sense. That is all AI requires.

Your First Success: The 10-Minute AI Prompt Challenge

Let's bypass the heavy technical definitions entirely and dive straight into a quick, real-world win. We aren't going to worry about deep theories today; we are just going to get your feet wet and show you immediate results in less than ten minutes.

We are going to open a basic AI chat tool. For this quick challenge, we will use ChatGPT. Please remember that the exact same language works beautifully whether you prefer Google Gemini or Microsoft Copilot. If you don't have a preferred tool yet, that is perfectly fine.

Let's walk through the setup together, step by step, with zero rush:

1. Prepare your screen: Requires a device and an internet browser.

Grab your laptop, tablet, or smartphone. If you are using a computer, open up the web browser you always use (such as Google Chrome, Apple Safari, or Microsoft Edge).

If you are using a tablet or smartphone, you can either open your internet browser or download the official, free app for your preferred assistant from your device's app store.

2. Go to the address or open the app: Navigating to the platform.

If you are on a computer, click the long address bar at the top of your screen, type exactly **chatgpt.com**, and press Enter. If you are using a mobile phone or tablet, simply tap open the app icon you just downloaded.

3. A simple sign-up: Creating your free account.

If you haven't used it before, the screen will ask you to create a free account. This is just like signing up for an online newspaper or a digital store layout - it will simply ask for your name and your email address. It might send a quick confirmation number to your email to verify it is you, which is a standard safety measure.

4. Locate the box: Finding the input field.

Once you are signed in, you will see a clean, simple page. At the very bottom, there is a large, empty box labeled "Send a message" or "Type here." That little box is our digital kitchen table.

Imagine the window looks just like this clean, simple layout illustrated in the notebook:

Now, click your mouse cursor directly into that big empty box, type the following sentence exactly as it is written, and press your "Enter" key (or click the little send arrow icon, which often looks like a small paper airplane > or an upward arrow next to the text field):

Give me three dinner ideas using chicken

Within just a few seconds, you will see the blank space fill with text as the AI responds to you in real time. Because the assistant builds its answers dynamically each time you type, the words look a little different for everyone. Still, it will deliver delicious, everyday options very much like this:

Chicken stir-fry with broccoli and bell peppers

Baked lemon herb chicken with roasted potatoes

Chicken tacos with avocado salsa

Look at that screen. Just like that, with one simple sentence, you are officially using AI for practical, real-world help.

But let's take it one step further to show you how conversational this tool really is. You don't need to start a new page or type a complex command. Just type a direct follow-up question into the box, as if you were speaking to a friend:

How do I make the baked lemon herb chicken?

Instantly, the tool will read the context of your conversation and provide clear, step-by-step cooking instructions for that exact recipe. It remembers exactly what it just suggested to you, so you don't need to retype the whole list. You can copy those ingredients directly onto your grocery list, text them to a friend, or write them on your kitchen whiteboard.

The good news is that you can completely customize this to fit your life. If you don't care for chicken, you can swap out the words seamlessly. Try clicking back into the box and typing something completely personal to your day:

Give me three dinner ideas using fish

Or perhaps you have a family event coming up:

Give me three birthday gift ideas for my granddaughter, who loves art

Every time you type, you will receive fresh, tailored ideas matched to your exact request. There is absolutely no penalty for trial and error here. You can ask as many questions as your heart desires - and if an answer ever feels a little off-topic or unhelpful, you can simply ignore it, rephrase your question, or ask it to try again. A small, gentle change in your wording is all it takes to unlock a completely clear answer.

Putting on Your "Supervisor Hat"

Now that you've seen the words appear on your screen, let's introduce the core mindset that will guide you through this entire book: **The Supervisor Hat**.

Think of the AI tool not as an all-knowing oracle, but as a wonderfully eager, incredibly fast, freshly hired summer intern. This intern has read millions of books and recipes, but they don't know you, they have no personal common sense, and they occasionally get a bit over-enthusiastic.

When you type a phrase into the text entry area, you are managing this intern. If they give you a recipe that calls for two cups of salt, or a historical date that feels incorrect to your memory, what do you do? You don't assume you are wrong; you put your hand on your hip, look at the intern, and say, "Let's check that again." You are always the supervisor in charge.

The Golden Rule of AI Safety: There is absolutely no way for you to "break" the AI by asking questions. You cannot push the wrong button, you cannot delete important files on your computer, and you cannot cause an error that can't be fixed by simply refreshing the page or closing the window.

To prove this to you, let's look at exactly how to handle the absolute worst-case scenarios you might encounter while typing.

WHEN AI ACTS UP
Don't Panic — Put On Your Supervisor Hat
Most AI problems have surprisingly simple solutions.
IF THIS HAPPENS...
WHAT IT ACTUALLY MEANS
YOUR SUPERVISOR ACTION
THE SCREEN FREEZES MID-SENTENCE.
Thinking...
The internet connection likely flickered for a moment.
Click the Refresh button in your browser
OR
Close the app and reopen it.
The assistant didn't forget you. It simply lost its connection.
THE ANSWER IS COMPLETELY UNHELPFUL.
INTERN
The intern misunderstood your goal or context.
Hmmm... I'm not sure what you need.
Type:
That's not quite what I meant. Let's try again, but focus only on..."
Bad answers usually need better directions, not a better computer.
A POP-UP SAYS "RATE LIMIT REACHED."
Rate Limit Reached
Please try again in a few minutes.
OK
The free system is simply busy with too many users.
Take a five-minute stretch break.
Pour a top-up of tea or coffee.
Wait five minutes.
ENTER
Try pressing Enter again.
Sometimes the assistant simply needs a short coffee break too.
STOP → CHECK → RETRY
Most AI hiccups are temporary.
A calm retry solves more problems than complicated troubleshooting.
Sticky-Note-To-Self
If something goes wrong:
1. Don't panic.
2. Read the message.
3. Try the simplest fix first.
4. Remember: you are the supervisor.
Small Problems. Simple Fixes. Confident Users.
Every experienced AI user has seen these messages before.

Reader Reviver Brain Break: The 20-20-20 Optic Reset

Before we move an inch further, let's practice our very first Digital Daisies Somatic Reset. Learning something brand new requires our brains to process new visual data, and staring intently at a screen can unconsciously tighten our shoulders and strain our eyes.

Let's push back from the keyboard for just sixty seconds:

The 20-20-20 reset: Look away from your computer, phone, or tablet screen right now. Find an object across the room or look out a window at something roughly 20 feet away. Rest your gaze on that object for 20 seconds. Feel your optic nerve completely relax.

The foot anchor: While you are looking away, place both feet flat on the floor. Feel the solid connection of the ground beneath you. Drop your shoulders down away from your ears, and let out a long, slow exhale.

Notice how that small physical pause clears the slight fog from your forehead? By lowering your body's subtle stress response, you instantly refresh your working memory. Now, with a calm mind, we can look at our progress.

Mini-Milestone: Reflect on Your First Prompt Win

Let's take a quick moment to celebrate what you have just accomplished in under ten minutes:

You successfully opened an online AI chat tool.

You typed an everyday request in plain English.

You secured a helpful, immediate answer.

You tinkered with your wording to see how the results changed.

If you have a notebook handy, take a brief moment to jot down your thoughts on these two simple reflection questions:

What surprised me the most about my very first AI prompt response?

What is one personal hobby or daily chore I want to try testing in the box next?

You have officially taken the single most important step of the entire journey: you have moved from simple curiosity about AI to using it for something meaningful in your real life. This is exactly how new skills form - small, comfortable actions that add up over time. You aren't forcing yourself to follow a rigid, confusing corporate script; you are gently shaping this technology to fit your unique lifestyle, one prompt at a time.

What Your Assistant Can (and Can't) Do for You

There is an incredible amount of loud noise and exaggeration surrounding artificial intelligence these days. It is completely natural to wonder what these tools actually do - and, more importantly, what they can realistically do for you in the real world.

Instead of viewing it as a mystery, let's look at the highly practical everyday tasks where your new digital intern truly excels, and where it hits a firm boundary.

Where the Assistant Excels

Polishing and Drafting Correspondence

If you need help drafting an email, polishing a rough letter, or finding the perfect phrase for a sensitive personal message, AI is an absolute lifesaver. For instance, if you need to cancel a medical appointment but find yourself struggling over the wording, you can simply ask,

"Draft a polite email to my dentist canceling my appointment for next Thursday." You will instantly receive a clean, ready-to-send draft that completely erases stress and overthinking.

Distilling Dense, Overwhelming Information

If you encounter a news article that is simply too long and dense to wade through, you can paste the text into the chat box and say, "Summarize this article in five sentences." The tool will instantly distill the text into a brief, easy-to-digest recap you can read in thirty seconds flat.

But it goes beyond the news. Imagine opening your email to find a massive, four-page legal update from your home appliance warranty company full of dense legalese. You can copy that wall of text, drop it into the box, and type: "Tell me in plain English: does this change cover my refrigerator repair, and what is the deadline?" The assistant will cut through the corporate jargon and pull out the exact nuggets of truth you actually need.

Organizing Layouts and Creative Outlines

For organizing logistics, it is unmatched. You can ask it to generate a practical packing list for a weekend driving trip to the mountains, create a structured checklist for a community volunteer meeting, or brainstorm fresh themes for your local book club. If you are exploring a brand-new hobby, it can break down complex concepts into gentle, step-by-step beginner study guides, or even quiz you on basic vocabulary if you are learning a new language.

The Firm Boundaries: What the Assistant Cannot Do

Because AI is not a living mind, it fundamentally operates like a clean whiteboard at the start of every fresh conversation. By default, it doesn't know your background, family relationships, or specific daily preferences unless you choose to provide them. It possesses no inner consciousness, holds no personal opinions or genuine human feelings, and relies entirely on the words you choose to feed into the box. It is a brilliant reflection engine that matches language patterns to give you the most helpful response possible based solely on the guidance you provide.

Café Notes: Practical, Everyday Inspiration

To give you a glimpse of what is possible as you begin to explore, look at how other adults are using these tools to bring ease and independence to their daily routines:

Community Organizers: "Write a brief announcement for our neighborhood association meeting about this month's guest speaker and the potluck details."

Grandparents: "Explain how photosynthesis works in simple, fun terms so I can explain it to my ten-year-old grandson during our walk tomorrow."

Gardeners and Crafters: "Suggest five companion plants for tomato bushes that help repel pests naturally in a small backyard plot," or "Create a 4-week beginner schedule for knitting a basic winter scarf."

Lifelong Learners: "Suggest three free online introductory resources or video channels for learning watercolor painting techniques."

As we wrap up our very first chapter, take a look at how far you've come already. You have opened the tool, sent your first commands, secured immediate successes, and learned exactly how to view your digital assistant through the lens of a confident supervisor. You are right where you need to be. Before you know it, that blinking cursor won't look like a challenge at all - it will look like a welcome invitation to create.

Whenever you are ready, let's turn the page to Chapter 2, where we will open the conversation about your privacy, show you how to handle data safely, and clear up any lingering questions about managing your personal information online.

Keeping Your Digital Space Private and Safe

Pull your chair in just a little bit closer and take another comfortable sip of your coffee. Now that you have secured your very first practical success in Chapter 1, that little entry box at the bottom of your screen probably feels a bit more like a helpful digital notebook and a lot less like an intimidating challenge. You know how to open the tool, you know how to type a basic question, and you have seen firsthand how quickly it responds with real, usable information.

Today, let's peel back the curtain just a little further. We are going to look at exactly how to step into your role as a manager, identify the tool's distinct boundaries, and - most importantly protect your personal privacy so you can explore this world with total peace of mind.

Most technology guides treat privacy like a dense legal contract, filled with terrifying warnings and endless corporate text that makes you want to close the book altogether. Let's do things differently.

Here is what really matters: AI is a marvelous tool. Like any good household appliance, it works best when you understand its built-in safety guards. You don't need to be a security expert to stay entirely safe. If you already know how to handle your everyday paper mail, you already have every single skill you need. When you drop a letter into a public mailbox, you ensure the envelope is sealed and that you haven't written a sensitive password on the back of the card. Managing your digital safety follows that exact same simple, common-sense rhythm.

The Core Boundaries: Spotting the Intern's Blind Spots

To prevent frustration, it is vital to understand where your virtual assistant hits a firm wall. Because AI can often sound remarkably human, intelligent, and confident, it is easy to assume it possesses a deep understanding of your life. But remember our core framework: it is an automated pattern-matcher, not a living mind. It does not look at our world with independent eyes; it simply guesses the next logical word in a sentence based on language patterns it has observed.

The machine encounters absolute limits in three specific areas:

1. Zero Personal Sight or Real-Time Awareness

Unless you explicitly provide details inside the text box during your current conversation, the AI knows absolutely nothing about you. It cannot access your private computer files, view your personal calendar, or read your emails.

Furthermore, unless a specific platform actively uses a live web search feature, its core knowledge has a fixed cutoff date. If you ask it for tomorrow's exact local weather forecast or who won last night's baseball game, it will usually give you a general answer or politely suggest checking a live news site. It is a companion for processing ideas, not a live news ticker.

2. No Professional or Medical Authority

While AI is wonderful at explaining a complex financial term in plain English or suggesting general wellness concepts, it is completely incapable of replacing a real, human professional. It cannot diagnose a specific medical symptom, provide official legal counsel, or manage your personal investments.

If you ask it for personalized medical advice, a responsible tool will return broad information and remind you to consult a qualified specialist. Treat it like a knowledgeable neighbor who can help you gather your thoughts and write down a clear list of questions before you sit down with your doctor, accountant, or attorney.

3. The Imaginative Streak (The "Hallucination")

This is the most important limitation to keep in mind as a supervisor. Because AI functions by predicting which words should logically follow one another, it would occasionally rather guess a plausible-sounding answer than simply put its hands up and admit it doesn't know the truth. This is known in the tech world as an **AI hallucination**.

The machine might give you a historical story that sounds incredibly authoritative, but completely mixes up a specific calendar year or invents a book title that never actually existed.

Never feel foolish if you catch the AI making a statement like this! It isn't a reflection of your prompting skill; it is just a quirk of the machine's predictive design.

The Supervisor Action: Always keep your manager's hat on. Treat the AI's output like a rough draft. Verify important historical facts, specific dates, or baking measurements before relying on them completely.

Reader Reviver Brain Break: The Security Exhale

Before we look at our simple privacy rules, let's take a brief moment to reset our physical bodies.

Talking about digital boundaries and security can cause us to unconsciously hold tension in our chests, necks, and jaws.

Let's practice a grounding Digital Daisies Reset right now:

The posture check: If you find yourself slouching forward toward your screen, gently roll your shoulders back and down. Imagine a soft string pulling the top of your head up toward the ceiling, lengthening your spine.

The security exhale: Place one hand gently on your stomach. Inhale slowly through your nose for a quiet count of four, letting your stomach expand like a balloon. Hold it for just a single second, and then let out a long, slow, rushing exhale through your mouth for a count of four.

The release: As you breathe out, completely relax your jaw, unclench your teeth, and let go of any tension lingering in your fingers and hands.

Notice how that small physical pause clears the slight fog from your forehead?

When your body breathes deeply, your brain instantly registers that you are in a safe space.

Now, with a calm, refreshed mind, let's look at how easy it is to keep your digital desk completely private.

Simple Privacy Guardrails: Staying Safe in the Digital Landscape

There is a lot of scary talk online about data security, but staying safe with AI is incredibly simple if you follow three plain-language rules.

When you open a free account with an AI tool, the parent company often uses the text of conversations in an anonymous form to help train its systems and make its language models smarter over time. Your specific name isn't posted on a public bulletin board. Still, because a human reviewer could theoretically look at sample texts to improve the system, you want to maintain a few healthy boundaries.

Think of it like sending a postcard through the mail - you wouldn't write your banking details where the mail carrier might glance at it. You would, however, happily write your holiday greetings, a story idea, or a recipe request.

Rule 1: Never Share Your Personal Identity Links

Never type passwords, credit card numbers, bank account details, or your Social Security number into an AI conversation box. The machine never needs this information to help you organize a project, write an email, or plan a trip. If a page ever prompts you for this data within the chat window, you are on the wrong website entirely.

Rule 2: Anonymize Your Drafts with Placeholders

If you are asking the AI to help you cut through dense information or polish a sensitive letter, simply leave the specific names and addresses blank or use generic placeholders.

Let's look at a real-world scenario. Imagine you have received a complicated, jargon-filled four-page insurance update regarding a property matter, and you want the AI to summarize it. Or perhaps you need to write a firm letter to a property manager. Instead of copying over the real names and specific account numbers, look at how we structure the prompt using simple placeholders:

Once the AI gives you the beautiful, polished text response, you simply copy that text out of the chat window and paste it into your own familiar word processor at home. Then, on your own device, you type the real names, specific dates, and street addresses safely. The AI handles the heavy lifting of the language, while your true records remain entirely at home on your own desk.

Rule 3: Use the "New Chat" Whiteboard Eraser

Every AI interface features a prominent button or icon designed to give you a clean slate. It is usually located in the top-left corner of the screen, labeled **"New Chat"** or **"New Topic,"** or represented by a simple plus sign +.

Clicking this completely clears the digital table. It closes the current visual conversation and opens a fresh, blank page.

Think of it like wiping a physical whiteboard completely clean with an eraser. If you have just spent 20 minutes working on a complex packing list for a trip and now want to switch to drafting a community volunteer flyer, clicking "New Chat" gives your assistant a fresh, uncluttered mind. It ensures that the background notes from your vacation planning don't bleed into or confuse the tone of the community document you are writing next.

Mini-Milestone: Your Personal Safety Checklist

Let's review the simple parameters that keep you entirely independent, secure, and in the driver's seat:

The Manager Role: You know that AI is a premium assistant for drafting, distilling, and organizing, but your common sense is always the final authority.

The Blueprint: You understand that AI can occasionally "hallucinate" details, meaning you always double-check recipes, dates, and hard facts.

The Mailbox Guard: You know how to keep your identity secure by using simple bracketed placeholders like [Name] instead of real personal information.

The Clean Slate: You know exactly how to use the "New Chat" button to wipe the whiteboard clean and keep your projects beautifully organized.

Take a brief moment to jot down a quick answer to this reflection prompt in your personal notebook:

What is one personal project (like organizing a cluttered recipe folder, summarizing a lengthy club newsletter, or drafting a flyer for a neighborhood potluck) that I can safely test today using a placeholder name?

Moving Forward with Confidence

Look at how much ground you have covered already! You have moved past the initial hesitation of the blank page, secured an immediate success with your first prompt, and mastered the basic everyday rules of digital safety. You aren't guessing or stumbling in the dark anymore; you have a clear, intentional framework for interacting with this modern landscape.

Whenever you are ready, let's turn the page to Chapter 3, where we will unlock the core engine of this entire book: **The Prompt Recipe**. We will learn how six simple, everyday ingredients can turn any generic AI response into a flawless, customized masterpiece on your very first try. Let's keep exploring!

Mastering the Core Engine

The Prompt Recipe

Settling back into our familiar corner with a fresh, warm mug, the digital landscape ahead suddenly looks a lot more inviting. By now, you have already broken the ice with your virtual assistant. You know how to safely navigate the screen, you understand how to protect your personal privacy using generic placeholders, and you have experienced that wonderful feeling of typing a simple phrase and getting an instant, helpful response.

Today, we are going to learn the single most important structural skill in this entire book. We are going to unlock the master key that turns AI from a generic, slightly robotic guessing machine into a brilliant personal assistant that responds exactly the way you want on the very first try.

In the technology world, engineers call this "prompt engineering." It sounds incredibly cold, academic, and intimidating, doesn't it? It makes it sound like you need a background in software construction or advanced mathematics just to get a clear answer from a computer screen. It evokes images of sterile computer science lecture halls and complex flowcharts.

Let's gently sweep that corporate language off our table.

Writing a truly great prompt is exactly like following a favorite, time-tested kitchen recipe. If you dump a handful of random ingredients into a bowl without any thought to measurements, timing, or temperature, you shouldn't be surprised if your cake comes out flat. But when you follow a simple, structured blueprint – adding just the right ingredients in just the right order – success becomes completely predictable. You are not changing how the computer programs operate under the hood; you are simply clarifying your instructions so the assistant does not have to guess your intentions.

The good news is that you only need to learn this formula once. We call it the **Prompt Recipe**. Once you understand its six simple ingredients, you can use it for every single task in this book, whether you are drafting a letter, organizing a vacation, or brainstorming a new hobby.

The Six Ingredients of the Prompt Recipe

Imagine you are standing at your kitchen counter, with six small bowls laid out in front of you. Each bowl holds one specific structural ingredient. You don't always have to use every single ingredient for every minor task, but when you combine them intentionally, you create a flawless digital outcome.

Let's look at the ingredients one by one, focusing on how they change the output on your screen:

The Role: Tell the machine exactly which "hat" it should wear before it begins typing. Because an AI has access to vast pools of language patterns, assigning it a specific role instantly narrows its focus. It tells the system exactly which library shelf to look at. For example: "Act as an experienced travel planner," or "Act as a patient, encouraging writing coach."

The Goal: This is the heart of your request. It is the clear, actionable task you want performed. Use strong, direct action words, such as: "Write a polite cancellation email," or "Create a balanced weekly meal plan."

The Context: Think of this as filling your assistant in on the background details before they start working. Providing the backstory leaves less room for the machine to make assumptions. For example: "I am planning a weekend driving trip for two adults in mid-October. We prefer scenic country roads and historical landmarks."

The Constraints: This is where you set the strict guardrails. You tell the AI exactly what to omit, how long the response should be, or which specific items to avoid. This prevents unnecessary paragraphs. For example: "Keep the response under 300 words. Do not include any seafood options. Avoid corporate jargon."

The Format: You don't have to accept a giant wall of messy text. You can dictate exactly how the information is arranged on your screen so it is easy on your eyes. For example: "Present the answer in a clean, numbered list," or "Organize the schedule into a simple table with columns for Time and Activity."

The Example: This is the secret weapon of great prompting. If you have a specific style or layout in mind, give the AI a small sample text of what you like. For example: "Write the response using a casual tone, similar to this: 'Hi neighbors, just a quick reminder that our annual block party is next Saturday!'"

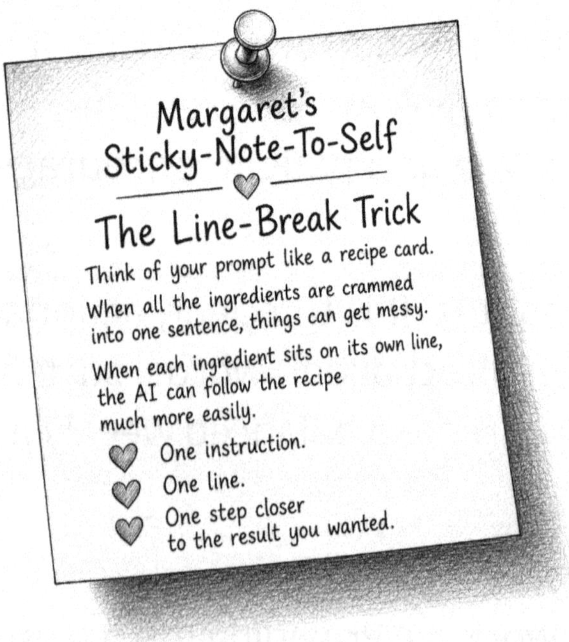

When you are typing a long Prompt Recipe into the input box, pressing the "Enter" key on your keyboard might accidentally send the message before you are finished typing all your ingredients! To prevent this, hold down the **Shift** key and press **Enter** together. This drops your cursor down to a fresh, clean line without sending the prompt, letting you build your recipe perfectly at your own leisure.

Reader Reviver Brain Break: The Cognitive Pause

Before we look at a real-world comparison of this recipe in action, let's practice a quick Digital Daisies Reset. When we are learning a structured framework, it is incredibly easy to start overthinking and tense up our minds.

Let's push back from the desktop for just sixty seconds:

The physical pause: Drop your hands completely off the keyboard or device and let them rest loosely in your lap.

The mind reset: Close your eyes or soften your gaze on the table in front of you. Take a deep, slow breath in through your nose, counting to four. Hold that breath for just two quiet counts. Now, open your mouth and let out a soft, sighing exhale for a count of four.

The intention: As you sit in this moment of stillness, remind yourself: I don't need to memorize all six ingredients right now. The blueprint is right here on the page whenever I need it.

Notice how that small physical pause clears the slight fog from your forehead? This brief cognitive pause ensures you approach the screen with calm, purposeful clarity, rather than a sense of rushed technical pressure.

The Recipe in Action: Before and After

To see why this structure is so incredibly powerful, let's look at the difference between a generic entry and a fully prepared Prompt Recipe using our established placeholder technique.

The Generic Approach

Imagine you type this simple sentence into the prompt box:

> Help me write a letter to my landlord about a broken kitchen pipe.

Because you didn't give the assistant any specific ingredients, it has to guess the tone, length, and intent. It will likely spit out an overly aggressive, multi-page legal brief that sounds like it was written by an expensive corporate attorney. It might automatically invoke housing codes or threaten escrow accounts, which doesn't match your personal style and certainly won't help maintain a friendly relationship with your landlord.

The Prompt Recipe Approach

Now, let's look at what happens when we mix our simple ingredients into the exact same request within the text box:

> "Act as a polite, firm, and respectful tenant. Write a brief letter to my landlord, [Landlord Name], requesting a repair. The cold-water pipe under my kitchen sink began leaking yesterday evening. I have turned the valve off and placed a bucket underneath, but it needs a professional plumber. Keep the letter under four sentences long. Use a courteous tone that maintains our good relationship without corporate jargon. Present it as a clean draft that I can easily copy."

By adding those clear pieces of information, the tool will instantly hand you a warm, beautifully balanced four-sentence note that states the problem clearly, respects your landlord's time, and protects your peace of mind – all on the very first try. You didn't have to sift through template letters or rewrite paragraphs to soften the edge. The ingredients did the work for you.

The Prompt Recipe Matrix

Use this layout as a visual map whenever you are building a new project. You can mix and match these lines depending on how complex your project is.

Troubleshooting Your Recipe Outcomes

Even with a recipe, an assistant can occasionally deliver an output that feels a little off-target. Because you have your supervisor hat on, you can instantly tune the output using **Iterative Grounding**—which just means giving a corrective note right in the current conversation without starting over.

If the output is too long or wordy: Don't retype the whole recipe. Simply type: "That's excellent, but please cut the length in half and present only the core steps as bullet points."

If the tone feels too stiff or robotic: Type: "Let's adjust the tone. Rewrite this version so it sounds like a warm, neighborly conversation over tea."

If it forgot a constraint: Type: "Remember, I cannot use a ladder. Please rewrite the gutter-cleaning instructions using only safety steps that keep my feet firmly on the ground."

Mini-Milestone: Celebrating Your New Skill

Let's pause and note exactly what you have mastered in this short chapter:

You learned that great prompting relies on clear, structured ingredients, not mysterious computer programming code.

You discovered how to use an explicit **Role** to give the assistant a focused perspective.

You learned how setting **Constraints** prevents the machine from drowning your screen in text.

You practiced a **Cognitive Pause** to clear away technical overthinking before you type.

Take a moment to write a quick answer to this reflection prompt in your personal notebook:

If I could assign any professional role to my AI assistant today (like a master chef, a professional home organizer, an antique appraiser, or an expert gardener), which one would be the most fun or helpful for me to explore next?

You have moved past basic experimentation and now hold the structural engine that makes technology work for you, entirely on your own terms.

Whenever you are ready, let's turn the page to Chapter 4, where we will enter Phase 2 of our journey and apply this exact Prompt Recipe to one of our most requested daily tasks: Writing and editing beautiful, polite emails and messages without a single drop of stress. Let's keep moving forward!

Writing and Editing

(Polite Emails & Clear Messages)

Stepping away from theory and moving straight into action, let's explore how these concepts fit comfortably into your everyday schedule. We are stepping into the practical application phase of our journey together. Now that you have the master blueprint of the Prompt Recipe tucked safely into your notebook, it is time to put it to work on one of the most persistent, time-consuming chores of modern life: handling our daily inbox.

Technology often promises to make communication faster, but it usually just makes it feel more stressful. Have you ever sat down to write what should be a simple message, only to find yourself staring at the screen for twenty minutes, typing a sentence, deleting it, rewriting it, and worrying about how your tone will be received?

Perhaps you need to bow out of a volunteer commitment without hurting anyone's feelings, ask a local contractor why a repair bill is higher than their initial estimate, or draft a firm note to a neighbor about their barking dog. We worry about sounding too blunt, or we write so much polite fluff that our actual point gets completely lost in the text. When you spend all your creative energy balancing on the tightrope of digital etiquette, a routine task begins to feel like an emotional burden.

The good news is that you don't have to bear the burden of finding the perfect words all by yourself anymore. Your virtual assistant is a masterful wordsmith. By deploying our Prompt Recipe, you can hand over your raw thoughts - no matter how messy or frustrated they might be - and watch your digital intern instantly polish them into an elegant, clear, and perfectly courteous message.

Tuning the Recipe Ingredients for Correspondence

When we use AI to help us write letters or messages, our goal as supervisors is to make sure the output sounds like a thoughtful, mature human being - not a sterile corporate lawyer, a pushy sales brochure, or a cold machine. To achieve this, we pick out the three specific structural ingredients that matter most for correspondence and tune them to protect our personal voice:

The Role (With Emotional Posture): Tell the AI exactly who it represents and the emotional attitude it should maintain. This sets the behavioral baseline. For example: "Act as a polite, community-minded neighborhood resident," or "Act as a warm, supportive grandmother."

The Context (The Raw Thought Dump): Give your assistant the raw facts and what has happened so far. Don't worry about grammar or elegance here - just dump the details out exactly as they come to your mind, including any rough notes or personal frustrations you want smoothed over.

The Constraints (Jargon-Pruning): This is your vital quality control tool. This is where we explicitly forbid robotic phrases or artificial text styles. For example: "Keep the email under two short paragraphs. Do not use corporate jargon or robotic catchphrases like 'I hope this email finds you well' or 'please do not hesitate to contact me.' Make it sound like a natural human spoke it."

Let's look at a quick example of how your raw, exhausted thoughts are transformed when passed through the Prompt Recipe filter inside the text window:

Reader Reviver Brain Break: The Scapular Tech-Neck Release

Before we look at our ready-to-use writing templates, let's check in with our physical bodies. When we focus intently on composing text or reading messages, we unconsciously enter a "tech slouch." Our neck drops forward, our chest collapses slightly, and our shoulder blades spread apart, which restricts our breathing and builds up physical tension.

Let's do a quick Digital Daisies Reset right now to open up your posture:

The Scapular Pinch: Sit up straight and tall in your chair, letting your arms hang loosely at your sides. Slowly roll your shoulders backward, and then imagine trying to pinch a pencil vertically between your two shoulder blades.

The Hold and Breathe: Hold that gentle pinch for five full seconds while taking a deep, slow breath in through your nose. Feel your chest fully expand and open.

The Drop: Exhale softly through your mouth and completely release the pinch, letting your shoulders drop down as far away from your ears as possible.

Repeat this sequence just twice. Notice how immediately the physical weight lifts from your upper back? More oxygen is flowing to your brain, your chest is open, and you are ready to command your screen with total clarity.

Real-World Writing Blueprints

Use these pre-arranged layouts to get pristine drafts on your very first try. Remember to use your bracketed placeholders [like this] for names and dates to keep your personal records completely on your own desk!

Blueprint 1: The Courteous Appointment Cancellation

Role: Act as a polite, responsible, and valued client.

Goal: Write a brief email to **[Recipient Name]** at the front desk, canceling my upcoming appointment on **[Date]** at **[Time]** due to an unexpected personal scheduling conflict.

Context: Ask for a list of available morning times next week so I can easily reschedule the visit.

Constraints: Keep the message to 4 sentences or fewer, ensure the tone is warm and professional, omit all stiff corporate jargon, and present it as a clean draft I can copy.

Blueprint 2: The Friendly Service Complaint

Role: Act as a kind, loyal, but observant customer.

Goal: Write a short, encouraging email to **[Owner Name]**, the manager of the local service business.

Context: Let them know that while their team did a wonderful job on the main project yesterday, the back corner near the **[Specific Location]** was accidentally left unfinished.

Constraints: Ask if they can swing back by sometime this week to touch it up. Keep the tone completely friendly, supportive, and firm - avoiding any angry words or clinical legal phrases.

Blueprint 3: The Graceful Boundary (Saying No)

Role: Act as a supportive, warm, but firm community member.

Goal: Write a short message to **[Name]** declining their invitation to take on the leadership role for the upcoming **[Event/Committee Name]**.

Context: Express my sincere gratitude for their thinking of me and reaffirm my support for the cause, but state clearly that I do not have the personal bandwidth to take on a major role right now.

Constraints: Keep it to two brief paragraphs, ensure the tone is gentle yet definitive, and avoid sounding like a generic corporate form letter.

When the AI gives you back a draft, remember that it is just a suggestion. It serves as your first rough copy, sitting on your digital kitchen table, ready for your final supervisory approval. If it uses a word that doesn't quite sound like your personal voice, you don't have to accept it. You can change it yourself in your word processor, or type a quick follow-up correction into the box like: "Make the second sentence sound a bit more casual," or "Shorten the ending." You remain the author; the machine is merely holding the pen.

Mini-Milestone: Reflecting on Your Communication Autonomy

Let's pause and note the incredible skills you have added to your toolkit in this chapter:

You learned how to use the Prompt Recipe to completely remove the anxiety of drafting tricky or sensitive emails.

You discovered how to use specialized **Constraints** to strip away cold, robotic, corporate phrases from your letters.

You used a **Scapular Tech-Neck Break** to physically reset your posture and open your chest while working.

You mastered using the assistant to set clear personal boundaries and decline requests gracefully without letting overthinking slow you down.

Take a brief moment to capture your thoughts on this reflection prompt in your personal notebook:

What is one email, message, or note sitting in my inbox right now that has been causing me a little bit of hesitation or procrastination? How can I apply a quick three-ingredient recipe to clear it out comfortably today?

Moving Forward with Total Confidence

You are doing absolutely beautiful work. By mastering the language of structured input, you have turned a daunting digital chore into a relaxed, streamlined process that takes minutes instead of hours. You have removed the guesswork from the empty text box and turned it into an active asset that works entirely on your terms.

Whenever you are ready, let's turn the page to Chapter 5, where we will use our assistant to master planning and organizing our schedules, packing lists, and dynamic menus with total ease. Let's keep exploring!

Planning and Organizing with Dynamic Layouts

Take a quick look at the surface of your desk or kitchen table right now. If your workspace looks anything like mine, there is a small pile of handwritten notes, torn calendar pages, and half-finished lists competing for your attention. Up to this point, we have used your assistant to handle outward communication – polishing letters and clearing out the emotional weight of a stressful inbox. Today, we are turning that engine inward to conquer the internal, invisible clutter of daily logistics: organizing schedules, building custom itineraries, and sorting real-world chaos into clean, beautiful order.

Today, we are going to look at how to use your assistant to tackle the heavy, exhausting mental lifting that comes with daily logistics. We are talking about planning and organizing.

Think about how much invisible energy we spend trying to organize the moving pieces of our lives. Imagine planning a week-long road trip: you have to keep track of driving distances, check what to pack for changing weather patterns, and remember to find charming local landmarks and diners along the way. Or think about the weekly routine closer to home: standing in front of an open refrigerator on a Tuesday afternoon, trying to invent a healthy dinner layout from three random ingredients while keeping a low-carbohydrate or low-salt constraint in mind.

This constant sorting creates **decision fatigue** - a very real state where your mind, forced to keep track of a dozen minor details at once, runs out of the energy needed for creative, peaceful thinking. Complex scheduling apps or heavy spreadsheet programs often add to the clutter, asking you to learn their technical entry formulas before they solve your problem.

The good news is that you don't need a complicated tracking app or an advanced digital calendar. Your AI assistant is a masterful logistical partner. By feeding your unique real-world needs into our trusted Prompt Recipe, you can get meticulously organized schedules, packing lists, and dynamic menus that make your life run smoothly.

Maximizing the Recipe: The Interplay of Context and Format

When we ask our assistant to organize a schedule, a menu, or a list for us, the secret to a flawless, stress-free result lies entirely in tuning two specific bowls of our Prompt Recipe: **Context** and **Format**.

The Context (The Ground Rules): Tell the assistant the exact parameters of your situation. Don't hold back details. If you are planning a trip, state who is going, how you prefer to travel, and your physical pacing limits. If you are planning a menu, list the exact ingredients you want to use up, as well as any dietary rules you must follow. The assistant handles the heavy computational rearranging, but your specific life details provide the framework.

The Format (The Grid Command): You never have to accept a messy, giant paragraph of text that strains your eyes. You can explicitly command the AI to arrange its response into a highly scannable, clean layout. You can dictate columns, bracketed check boxes, or bold conceptual blocks.

Let's look at a real-world comparison to see how a simple change in your Format ingredient completely changes how information hits your eyes:

Reader Reviver Brain Break: The Finger-Tap Rhythm Cadence

Before we look at our real-world planning templates, let’s check in with our hands and wrists. When we type out logistics or scroll through dense digital schedules, our fingers and hands can develop significant repetitive muscle tension.

Let's do a brief Digital Daisies Reset to bring a burst of fresh blood flow and physical rhythm back to your hands:

The Keyboard Release: Drop both hands completely away from your device, and let your arms rest comfortably on your lap or on the tabletop.

The Thumb Touch: Tap your right thumb firmly against your index finger. Now tap it to your middle finger, your ring finger, and your pinky finger. Move back up the line: pinky, ring, middle, index.

The Sync: Repeat this identical tapping rhythm with your left hand. Now, try doing both hands at the exact same time, creating a steady, comforting rhythm.

The Slow Exhale: As you tap your fingers sequentially, take a slow, deep breath in through your nose for a count of four, and let out a gentle, soft, sighing exhale through your mouth.

Stop tapping, open your hands wide, spread your fingers for 3 seconds, then let them go completely loose. This physical, tactile exercise entirely resets your neurological focus, breaks up posture strain, and clears your short-term memory so you can return to your screen completely refreshed.

Real-World Planning Blueprints

Use these pre-configured layouts to bring immediate, structural organization out of daily chaos. Remember to use your bracketed placeholders to keep your specific personal plans completely private!

Blueprint 1: The Balanced Road Trip Itinerary

Role: Act as an expert, relaxed personal travel planner.

Goal: Create a detailed 3-day driving itinerary for two mature adults traveling from **[Starting Location]** to **[Destination]** in **[Month]**.

Context: We want to drive no more than two hours per day, avoiding busy interstate highways in favor of scenic coastal or country roads. Include one historical landmark and one quiet, local diner recommendation for each individual day.

Constraints: Keep the tone completely warm and practical. Avoid crowded tourist traps.

Format: Organize the final answer into a clean, easy-to-read table with clear columns for: 'Day', 'Suggested Route', 'Stop Over', and 'Dining Idea'.

Blueprint 2: The Weather-Specific Packing Template

Role: Act as a meticulously organized personal packing assistant.

Goal: Create a complete packing checklist for a **[Number]**-day weekend trip to a **[Location Type]** in **[Season]**.

Context: The forecast predicts daytime temperatures of **[Temperature]** degrees and a high chance of **[Weather, e.g., rain/snow]**. The traveler enjoys light walking and cozy evenings indoors.

Constraints: Group the items logically into four distinct, scannable categories: 'Essential Electronics & Documents', 'Clothing & Layers', 'Outdoor Gear', and 'Comfort Items'.

Format: Present this as a clean, printable bulleted list, with empty brackets [ ] next to each item, so I can check them off manually with a pen.

Blueprint 3: The Refrigerator Clean-Out Menu

Role: Act as a practical, highly resourceful home chef.

Goal: Give me three healthy dinner ideas based exclusively on these specific ingredients currently sitting in my kitchen: **[Ingredient 1]**, **[Ingredient 2]**, and **[Ingredient 3]**.

Context: I already have standard pantry staples like olive oil, garlic, salt, and pepper available.

Constraints: Please ensure all three meal ideas are entirely **[Dietary rule, e.g., low-carbohydrate/low-sodium] and require less than 30** minutes of active cooking time.

Format: Present each of the three options with a bold title, followed immediately by a brief, three-step list of clear cooking instructions.

Sticky Note to Self: Moving Tables Off-Screen

If your digital intern generates a table or a checklist layout that you absolutely love, you don't need to feel trapped looking at it inside the chat tool window forever. Simply click and drag your mouse cursor to highlight the entire grid, right-click, and select "Copy," then paste it straight into a standard blank word processing document or an email draft on your computer. It will preserve its clean grid lines and check boxes perfectly, allowing you to print it safely for your refrigerator, home planner, or clipboard.

Mini-Milestone: Reflecting on Your Analytical Order

Let's take a quick moment to look at the powerful structural order you have brought into your world during this short chapter:

You learned how to use the Prompt Recipe to actively combat decision fatigue by offloading complex coordination tasks.

You discovered how to use the **Format** ingredient to command the AI to build clean, custom grids and checklists that are easy on your eyes.

You used a **Finger-Tap Cadence Break** to physically relieve muscle strain away from the keyboard and reset your working memory.

You mastered feeding highly specific real-world context into the ext window to unlock custom solutions for your kitchen and your travels.

Take a brief moment to write down your response to this reflection prompt in your notebook:

What is one upcoming event, family dinner, or weekend activity that has been swirling around in my mind? How can I apply a clear table format prompt to organize its moving pieces comfortably today?

Moving Forward with Total Confidence

You are doing absolutely marvelous work. By matching your deep life experience with clear structural instructions, you have transformed your AI assistant into an incredibly high-utility logistical tool that works entirely on your terms.

You have successfully shifted from being a passive note-taker to an active supervisor of information layouts. The heavy mental sorting is officially off your shoulders. Close your notebook for a brief moment, let your eyes wander away from the desk, and whenever your mind feels completely rested and clear, let's step into our next workspace together to explore how to instantly dismantle long, dense online articles on your own terms.

Summarizing and Parsing

(Taming Long Articles & Reports)

Think back to the last time you clicked on a fascinating historical article, a local community report, or a family email, only to be met by a literal fortress of text – twenty dense paragraphs packed with corporate padding, repetitive dates, and academic fluff. Your eyes strained, your attention drifted, and you simply wanted the core points without wading through the swamp. That invisible mental exhaustion is called information overload, and today, we are going to teach your lightning-fast reader how to dismantle it in under thirty seconds flat.

Think about how much dense text we are expected to digest every single day. Imagine clicking on a fascinating news story, a historical report, or a community association update, only to find yourself staring at a literal wall of words - twenty paragraphs of tiny text packed with heavy, academic padding and repetitive details.

Your eyes strain, your attention drifts, and you just want to know the main point without wasting twenty minutes reading through it all. Or perhaps a well-meaning friend emails you a lengthy, multi-page report about a local development plan, or you find a long historical essay online related to a hobby you love.

You want the core knowledge, but you don't want the screen fatigue that comes with wading through the fluff.

Sifting through excessive text just to find a single date or a core decision is an exhausting drain on your morning energy.

The good news is that you don't have to bear the burden of reading every single word yourself anymore.

Your AI assistant is a brilliant, lightning-fast reader.

By using a tailored version of our Prompt Recipe, you can hand over any long, jargon-heavy article and watch the machine instantly distill it into a brief, clear, and perfectly readable summary - all in under thirty seconds flat.

The recipe ingredients for crisp summaries

When we use AI to parse and condense text, the secret to a high-utility result lies entirely in our Constraints and Format bowls. If we don't set explicit boundaries, the assistant will simply give you back another long, wordy paragraph that strains your eyes.

Here is how we adjust our kitchen ingredients to get a perfectly crisp recap:

The role: Give the AI a highly precise, efficient, and plain-spoken mindset. This tells the tool to look at the text through an editorial lens. For example: "Act as an expert, concise research assistant," or "Act as a clear, plain-English news editor."

The context: This is simply the text you want parsed. You don't need to clean it up or format it; you just hand the raw document over to the assistant.

The constraints: This is where you enforce the law of brevity. You explicitly command the machine: "Summarize the text using absolute plain English. Strip out all repetitive filler, corporate fluff, and unnecessary background dates."

The format: Dictate exactly how you want your eyes to receive the data. Instead of blocks of text, demand scannable structures.

Tell the machine: "Present the summary in exactly five short, distinct bullet points," or "Give me a single-sentence headline followed by three quick highlights."

Reader Reviver Brain Break: The bilateral eye movement reset

Before we open up our summarization blueprints, let's practice a unique Digital Daisies Reset designed specifically to relieve visual processing fatigue. Staring intently at dense blocks of text causes our eye tracking muscles to lock up and strains our short-term memory.

Let's push back from the desktop for just sixty seconds:

The fixed base: Sit up straight and keep your head completely still, facing forward. Let your chin rest comfortably, and look straight ahead at the wall across from you.

The horizontal track: Without moving your head a single inch, slowly glide your eyes as far to the right as they can comfortably go. Hold your gaze there for three seconds, feeling the gentle stretch.

The left glide: Smoothly glide your eyes all the way across the room to the far left. Hold your gaze there for three seconds.

The rhythmic flow: Gently track your eyes back and forth from right to left, five times sequentially, at a slow, steady, and relaxed pace.

The soft close: Close your eyes completely. Take a deep, slow breath in through your nose, counting to four, and let out a long, sighing exhale as you let your eyelids rest in total darkness for ten seconds.

Open your eyes gently. Notice how much brighter and clearer the room looks? This simple lateral movement stimulates bilateral brain activity, releases tension in the tiny tracking muscles of your eyes, and instantly lifts the visual fog caused by reading dense digital text.

To copy a long article into the AI box, you don't need to worry about losing your place or messing up the alignment. Simply click your mouse at the top of the article, hold down the mouse button, and drag it all the way to the bottom to highlight the text, right-click to select

"Copy," then right-click inside your AI prompt box and select "Paste." Even if the text looks messy or runs together in the box, the machine's pattern-matcher will read it perfectly.

Real-world summarization blueprints

Use these functional frameworks to instantly tame overwhelming walls of text. You can copy these precise layouts directly into your assistant today:

Summarization style

Blueprint recipe template

1. News Highlight Recap

> **Role:** Act as a clear, plain-English news editor.

Goal: Summarize the long article attached below.

Context: [Paste your text here]

Constraints: Strip out all repetitive background details and corporate filler. Ensure each point is written in simple, everyday language.

Format: Please organize the final answer into exactly five short, distinct bullet points.

2. The "TL;DR" Overview

> **Role:** Act as an exceptionally efficient personal research assistant.

Goal: Review the lengthy text below and provide a "TL;DR" summary.

Context: [Paste your text here]

Constraints: Keep the tone completely direct and clear.

Format: Give me one single, bold sentence that explains the absolute main takeaway, followed by a bulleted list of three specific action items or dates that require attention.

3. Technical Jargon Translator

> **Role:** Act as a patient, knowledgeable teacher.

Goal: Review the dense report attached below.

Context: [Paste your text here]

Constraints: Translate the core message into simple, warm language that an absolute beginner can understand. Completely remove any complex legal or technical jargon, replacing those phrases with everyday analogies.

Format: Present the final answer as two short, readable paragraphs.

Mini-milestone: Reflecting on your information mastery

Let's pause and note the incredible layer of digital autonomy you have secured in this chapter:

You learned how to use the Prompt Recipe to completely eliminate information overwhelm and decision fatigue.

You discovered how to command the AI to strip out academic padding and corporate jargon using strict Constraints.

You used a Bilateral Eye Movement Break to relieve visual processing fatigue away from the monitor.

You explored how to use specific structural settings to extract instant, single-sentence headlines from dense documents.

Take a brief moment to jot down a quick answer to this reflection prompt in your notebook:

What is one lengthy article, online clipping, or community document I have been avoiding because it looks too long to read? How can I use a five-bullet summary prompt to conquer it today?

Moving forward with total confidence

You are doing absolutely marvelous work. By turning your virtual assistant into a dedicated, plain-English editor, you have taken complete control over your time and protected your cognitive energy from modern digital noise.

You have removed the stress of wading through corporate fluff and academic padding, letting the facts stand out clearly on your own terms. You are moving at the perfect pace, and your independence is entirely real.

By converting your assistant into a plain-English editor, you have safely built a protective shield around your daily time and cognitive energy. Information now stands on your table strictly on your own terms. Rest your arms comfortably, roll your neck out slowly, and let this module settle completely into your memory before we move our chairs over to our next collaborative workbench.

A Plate of Warm Scones

***** REVIEW*****

Every new skill begins with a single step – and your review could be the spark that encourages someone else to start

their own journey. When you share your thoughts, you're offering reassurance that whispers: "If they can do it, maybe I can too!"

Think of it as leaving a trail of breadcrumbs – or perhaps a plate of warm scones – so that fellow learners feel confident to sit down next to you and start learning.

By sharing your honest review, you help to:

Inspire confidence in other beginners

Keep the learning conversation alive and thriving

Build a warm, supportive community of explorers

Thank you for being part of this journey. The real magic of AI Prompts isn't just in what they can achieve – it's in how we use them together, passing along discoveries like stories shared over a warm brew.

Please leave your review on the platform where you found this book, or use this link:

[https://www.amazon.com/review/review-your-purchases/?asin=BOOKASIN]

Warmly,
Margaret Fields
Author of The **Digital Daisies & Curious Bytes** series: AI for Beginners Over Fifty and ChatGPT For Beginners Over Fifty

Creative Brainstorming and Sparking Fresh Ideas

Up to this exact moment, we have used your digital intern for heavy, logical chores – clearing out stressful correspondence, tracking messy travel variables, and parsing walls of dense text. Those are the essential, protective boundaries that secure your personal freedom.

So, today, we are leaving the rigid rules of organization behind and stepping into a wide, open playground where your assistant ceases to be an administrative clerk and becomes an imaginative, non-judgmental creative partner.

Today, we are shifting our focus entirely. We are going to look at how to use your assistant as an active, imaginative partner to unlock fresh waves of creativity and exploration in your everyday life.

Think about those moments when you want to step outside your usual routine but find yourself stuck in a creative rut.

Perhaps you are looking for a completely unique, thoughtful theme for your local book club's next meeting. Maybe you are searching for a fresh, personalized gift idea for a family member who seems to already have everything. Or perhaps you have a quiet dream of diving back into a creative hobby – like journaling, memory keeping, or writing short stories. Then you find yourself staring blankly at the page, waiting for inspiration to strike.

Traditional technology often stifles creativity by burying us in an endless maze of internet search results, pop-up advertisements, and chaotic forums. When you are looking for a spark of inspiration, scrolling through millions of scattered opinion pieces or retail advertisements can quickly drain your creative energy.

The good news is that your AI assistant functions beautifully as a vibrant garden that grows ideas. Because it holds no personal ego, never gets tired, and possesses immediate access to millions of historical, literary, and artistic concepts, you can use it to jump-start your imagination.

By feeding your natural curiosity into our trusted Prompt Recipe, you can instantly generate tailored, creative concepts that add a burst of fun and discovery to your world. It acts as an open-minded sounding board that will happily explore a hundred different whimsical angles with you, never making you feel rushed or silly for testing an unconventional idea.

Tuning the Recipe for a Creative Spark

When we ask our assistant to act as a creative collaborator rather than a strict logical assistant, we want to pick out ingredients that invite the machine to step away from predictable corporate text patterns. This relies entirely on matching an imaginative **Role** with a technical constraint known as the **Anti-Cliché Valve**.

The Role (Imaginative Personas): Tell the assistant to step away from the dry, administrative clerk persona. Command it to approach your question with the warmth, depth, and resourcefulness of a human artisan. For example: "Act as an inventive, warm event designer," or "Act as a patient, encouraging childhood memoir coach."

The Constraints (The Anti-Cliché Valve): By default, an unguided AI will often suggest the most common, predictable ideas found on the internet because those are the most frequent language patterns it knows.

To get true innovation, you must explicitly tighten the valve. You do this by telling the machine exactly what not to suggest. For example: "Avoid predictable, overused clichés or commercial store-bought solutions. Focus exclusively on tactile, hands-on, historical, or sensorially rich experiences."

Let's look at how adding an explicit Anti-Cliché Valve changes the creative output on your screen:

Reader Reviver Brain Break: The Creative Horizon Stretch

Before we explore our creative blueprints, let's check in with your physical body.

Sitting at a computer or holding a mobile tablet for too long can cause our lower back to tighten and our posture to freeze, which physically shuts down our creative, lateral thinking.

Let's do a quick Digital Daisies Reset to open up your torso and refresh your physical perspective:

The Planted Base: Sit comfortably upright in your chair, with both feet placed flat on the floor. Let your hands rest loosely and heavily on your knees.

The Seated Twist: Take a slow, deep breath in through your nose, consciously lengthening your spine toward the ceiling.

As you exhale softly through your mouth, gently twist your upper body to the right, placing your left hand on your right thigh and looking over your right shoulder toward the far wall.

The Center Breath: Hold this soft stretch for three seconds, breathing easily into your rib cage. Slowly unwind back to the center.

The Counter Twist: Inhale deeply again, and as you exhale, gently twist your upper body to the left, placing your right hand on your left thigh and looking over your left shoulder.

Hold for three seconds, and then return smoothly to the center.

Let out a long, clearing sigh and loosen your arms. This simple movement gently stretches your lower back, opens up your rib cage for deeper breathing, and physically pulls your awareness away from the flat desktop, signaling your brain that it is safe to play, explore, and think creatively.

Real-World Brainstorming Blueprints

Use these imagination catalysts to bring fresh, creative energy to your hobbies and gatherings. Remember to use your bracketed placeholders to customize the raw context to match your true family circle!

Blueprint 1: The Immersive Book Club Gathering Theme

Role: Act as an inventive, warm, and highly thoughtful event designer.

Goal: Generate three unique, cohesive meeting themes for our neighborhood book club's next gathering.

Context: We are currently reading a **[Genre/Era, e.g., historical mystery novel set in London during the 1920s]**. For each theme, provide a catchy title, a suggestion for a simple, era-appropriate beverage or snack, and two fun, out-of-the-box discussion icebreaker questions.

Constraints: Avoid common, predictable party clichés or generic plastic decorations. Focus on immersive, sensory elements. Keep the tone completely warm and welcoming.

Format: Organize the final answer with clean headings and bullet points.

Blueprint 2: The Meaningful Milestone Gift Discovery

Role: Act as a deeply thoughtful, highly perceptive personal gift consultant.

Goal: Brainstorm five unique, meaningful gift ideas for an upcoming milestone celebration.

Context: The recipient is celebrating a **[Milestone, e.g., 70th birthday]**. She has a busy life but loves **[Hobby 1, e.g., quiet gardening]**, **[Hobby 2, e.g., classic literature]**, and **[Hobby 3, e.g., baking heirloom sourdough bread]**. She values high-utility tools, personal keepsakes, or hands-on experiences.

Constraints: Avoid generic clothing gift cards, standard flowers, or digital gadgets. For each idea, explain briefly why it connects to the recipient's passions and how I can personalize it.

Format: Present this as a clean, numbered list with plenty of white space between each suggestion for easy reading.

Blueprint 3: The Memory & Journaling Starter

Role: Act as a patient, encouraging creative writing coach.

Goal: Provide three distinct, evocative writing prompts or journal starters to help me capture and record stories from my youth.

Context: Focus the prompts heavily around specific sensory details – such as the unique sounds of a childhood kitchen, the memory of a favorite family holiday trip, or learning a traditional manual skill like **[Skill, e.g., quilting / carpentry]** from an older relative.

Constraints: Keep the instructions for each individual starter to exactly three sentences long. Maintain a tone that is completely inviting and pressure-free, ensuring they inspire joyful curiosity rather than writing anxiety.

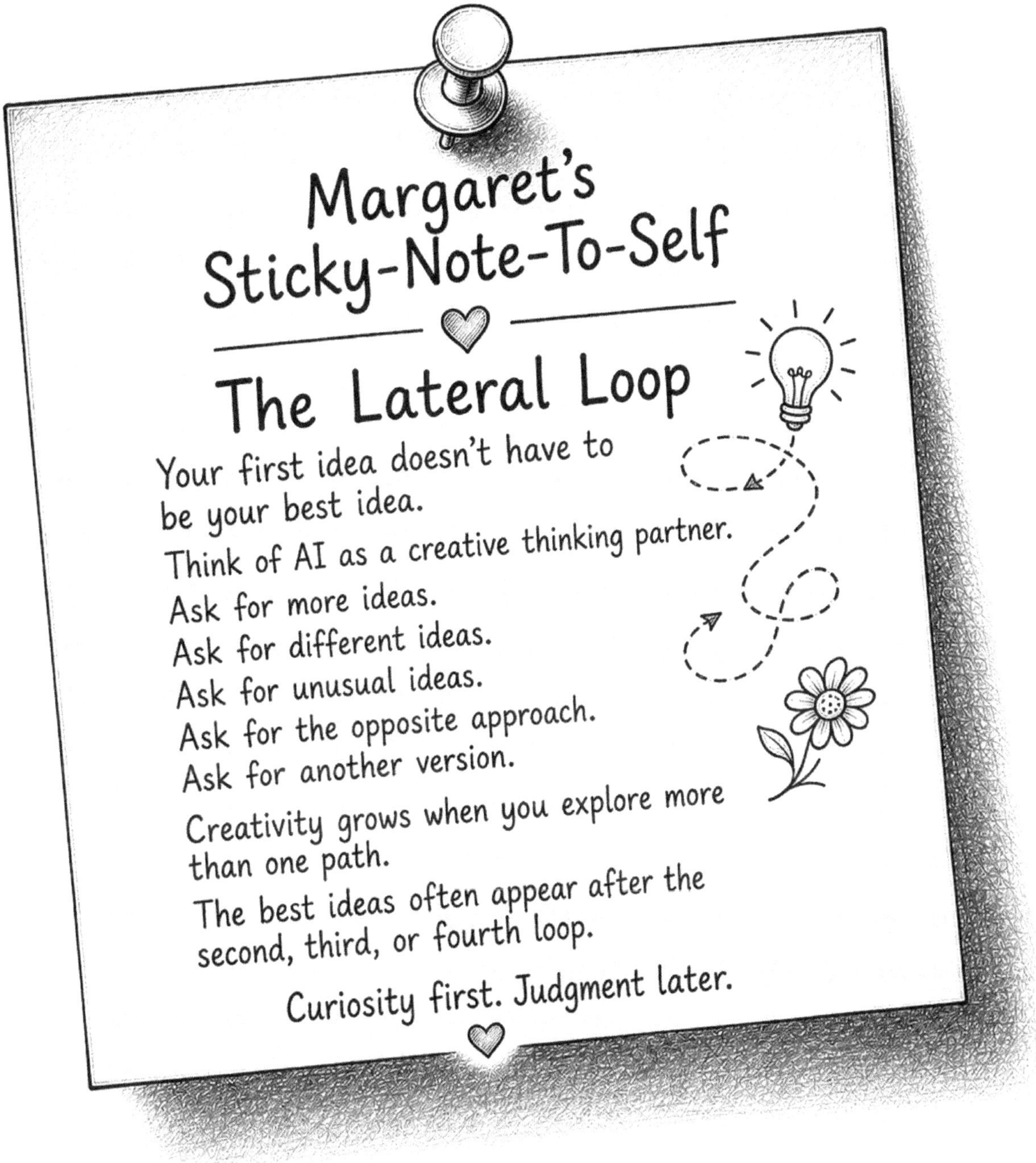

When brainstorming, you don't have to stop after the first answer! Treat your assistant like a conversational tennis partner.

If the AI gives you five gift ideas and number three catches your eye, simply type back: "I love idea number three, but let's dive deeper into just that concept. Give me three specific ways I can construct or package that particular idea at home using basic materials." The assistant will happily narrow its focus and keep brainstorming along that exact thread with you.

Mini-Milestone: Reflecting on Your Creative Momentum

Let's pause and note the wonderful structural milestones you have achieved in this chapter:

You learned how to transform your assistant from a rigid task manager into an active, imaginative partner for your hobbies.

You discovered how to implement the **Anti-Cliché Valve** constraint to filter out boring internet tropes in favor of original concepts.

You used a **Creative Horizon Stretch** to physically relieve torso strain, open up your breathing, and refresh your mind for lateral thinking.

You mastered using the prompt entry window to easily spark personalized ideas for family gifts, club themes, and sensory-focused memoir writing.

Take a brief moment to capture a quick response to this reflection question in your personal notebook:

What is one creative hobby, hand-crafted project, or personal writing idea I have put on the back burner lately? How can I apply a playful three-ingredient recipe to uncover a fresh, simple entry point into it this week?

Moving Forward with Total Confidence

You are doing absolutely magnificent work. By bringing your deep well of life experience to the prompt table, you have unlocked the true potential of this technology—treating it as a collaborative partner that respects your intelligence and enhances your creative freedom. You have transitioned from using the box for basic, repetitive tasks to using it as an active companion for storytelling, exploration, and joy.

You have officially moved past basic utility commands and discovered how to treat the empty text field as a collaborative canvas for exploration. Your life experience is now actively shaping new ideas. Slip your notebook into your drawer, stretch your fingers wide for three seconds, and let your mind relax into a quiet space before we dive into the deep, personal world of preserving your family history.

Preserving Your Digital Legacy and Family History

Settle back into your favorite corner, take a slow, comforting sip of your coffee, and let's look at a deeply personal way to align this technology with your heart. Up to this point, we have used your virtual assistant to handle the immediate, structured friction of modern life: smoothing out stressful emails, tracking neighborhood logistics, and instantly parsing heavy blocks of online text. Those are the defensive chores that preserve your time.

Today, we are moving into the creative space where you get to put that newly reclaimed time to beautiful use. We are going to look at how to transform your assistant from a simple administrative clerk into an attentive family scribe - a patient companion to help you organize old photographs, preserve ancestral memories, and structure your personal history into beautiful, lasting narratives to pass down to future generations.

Think about the physical weight of memory that many of us carry in our homes. Perhaps you have a cedar chest in the attic filled with decades of uncataloged family photographs, or a desk drawer crowded with yellowed letters, recipes written in your grandmother's handwriting, and old newspaper clippings. Maybe you have spent years promising yourself that you would finally write down the stories of your childhood, the memories of your early career, or the history of how your family arrived in your hometown.

Traditional technology makes the beautiful act of preserving family history look like a grueling data-entry project. Most ancestral websites and digital archiving programs throw you into a maze of cold spreadsheets, rigid family trees, and complicated scanning software that leaves you feeling overwhelmed before you can even locate a single date.

Let's change the approach entirely. You do not need to be a professional archivist or a database manager to rescue your family stories from the fog of time. Effective prompting is a learnable skill rather than a technical talent, and experimentation, curiosity, and small improvements will always serve you better than chasing immediate perfection.

Your AI assistant is a brilliant listener and a highly organized text coordinator. By using a tailored version of our Prompt Recipe, you can hand over raw, disjointed recollections - just the scattered thoughts, loose dates, and family names exactly as you remember them - and watch the machine instantly polish them into a beautifully structured chronological timeline, a narrative chapter, or an organized indexing grid.

The Recipe Ingredients for Family Archiving

When we use AI to help preserve histories and memories, our standard kitchen recipe adapts to prioritize emotional warmth, absolute historical precision, and visual order. We want to avoid generic, romanticized fiction; instead, we want the machine to respect your authentic voice and protect the exact facts of your life. Think of this process as a series of low-pressure experiments where you retain full creative control.

To achieve this, we pick out specific ingredients that establish firm guardrails:

The Role: Give the AI a highly respectful, patient, and precise historical mindset. This ensures the tone remains dignified, warm, and clear, rather than sounding like a sensationalized magazine article. For example: "Act as an encouraging personal biographer," or "Act as a meticulous family history archivist."

The Context: This is where you share your raw memories or file descriptions without worrying about grammar or structure. You can type in running thoughts, names of relatives, approximate decades, and specific sensory details, such as the rhythmic clack of an old screen door, the hum of heavy machinery in a workshop, or the sharp aroma of woodsmoke and a holiday kitchen.

The Constraints: This is your vital quality control tool - your authenticity guardrail. You explicitly command the assistant to stick strictly to the facts you provide, avoiding any artificial elaboration, fabricated research, or invented details. Tell the machine: "Do not invent any historical background or add flowery prose. Keep the language entirely natural, honest, and reflective. Retain my unique vocal style."

The Format: Command the AI to deliver highly scannable, usable structures. If you are tracking old photo albums, demand a clean grid layout. If you are writing down memories, ask for short, readable paragraphs with plenty of space between them.

Reader Reviver Brain Break: The Heart-Opening Desk Stretch

Before we look at our ready-to-use family history templates, let's check in with our physical bodies. When we reflect on deeply personal memories or spend time typing out ancestral details, our emotional focus can cause us to unconsciously pull our chest forward and drop our chin down toward our collarbone, tightening the delicate muscles around the heart and upper spine.

Let's push back from the desktop for just sixty seconds to open up your torso and invite a deep breath into your frame:

The Seated Base: Sit upright and tall in your chair, letting your arms hang loosely at your sides. Ensure both feet are resting flat on the floor, anchoring your posture.

The Shoulder Roll: Inhale slowly through your nose for a count of four while lifting your shoulders up toward your ears. Roll them backward, down, and away from your neck as you exhale softly.

A Chest Expansion: Interlace your fingers behind your lower back if comfortable. Gently pull your hands down toward the chair cushion, drawing your elbows toward each other. Feel a beautiful, broad expansion stretch across the front of your chest and shoulders.

The Deep Intake: Hold this gentle opening stretch for three slow, steady breaths. Inhale deeply through your nose, letting your ribs expand wide, and let out a long, quiet, sighing exhale through your mouth.

Release your fingers, return your hands to your lap, and let your shoulders drop down. Notice how immediately the physical weight lifts from your upper frame? This simple somatic exercise opens up your rib cage, floods your brain with fresh oxygen, and resets your visual memory so you can return to your project feeling completely grounded, spacious, and calm.

Real-World Legacy Blueprints

Use these functional frameworks to easily transform raw memories and scattered records into beautifully organized family treasures. You can copy these precise layouts directly into your assistant today:

Blueprint 1: The Memory Polisher

Use this framework to turn a chaotic memory or an unedited stream of recollections into a beautifully paced narrative chapter.

Role: Act as a warm, encouraging personal biographer and oral historian.

Goal: Transform the raw, disjointed family memory attached below into a clean, beautifully written narrative chapter.

Context: [Paste or type your raw running thoughts about a specific memory here, including names and places].

Constraints: Retain my authentic first-person voice. Do not add any invented dialogue, fabricated historical background, or flowery filler. Keep the tone dignified, reflective, and completely natural. Focus heavily on the real-world sensory details provided in my text.

Format: Present the final narrative in three to four short, readable paragraphs with generous spacing.

Blueprint 2: The Photo Album Archiver

Use this framework to bring physical order to unorganized boxes of old photographs before they are lost to time.

Role: Act as a meticulously organized family history archivist.

Goal: Create a structured cataloging grid to help me systematically document and label a box of unorganized family photographs.

Context: I am cataloging miscellaneous loose photos spanning from the late 1940s through the mid-1970s, featuring various family branches, holiday gatherings, and travel locations.

Constraints: Keep the column names practical and clear for manual data entry. Avoid complex digital cataloging jargon.

Format: Organize the final response into a clean, easy-to-read table with separate columns for 'Box/Album Number', 'Approximate Year', 'People Pictured', 'Location', and 'Special Notes or Clues'.

Blueprint 3: The Biographer's Interview

Use this framework when you face a blank page and need a gentle, step-by-step spark to get your memories flowing.

Role: Act as a gentle, patient family historian and interviewer.

Goal: Act as a supportive writing partner to help me systematically recall and document my early childhood memories.

Context: I want to write down stories from my youth to share with my grandchildren, but I am facing a blank page and do not know where to start.

Constraints: Ask me exactly five distinct, thought-provoking questions focused strictly on sensory details from a childhood home, such as family kitchens, holiday traditions, or neighborhood sounds. Do not overwhelm me; present all five questions at once in simple English.

Format: Present the final set of questions as a clean, spaced, numbered list.

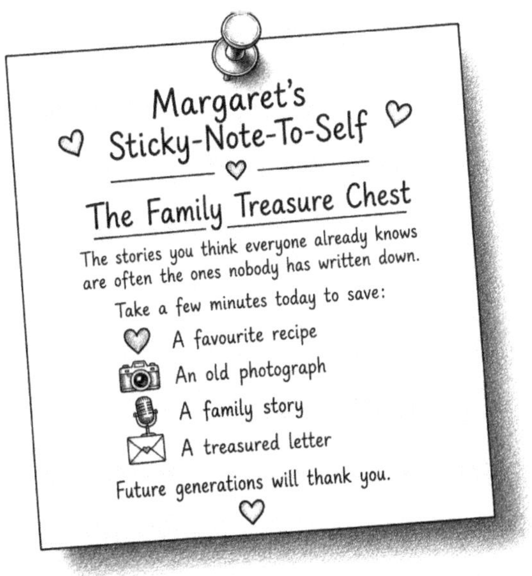

If typing out your raw memories ever feels tedious or makes your fingers stiffen up, remember that you don't have to use the keyboard. If your tablet or smartphone has a microphone icon on the keyboard screen, tap it and simply tell your story aloud, as if you were speaking to an old friend over coffee. Let your thoughts wander, pause to think, and don't worry about being orderly. Your assistant will catch the text perfectly, and your Prompt Recipe will handle the organization later.

The Recipe in Action: Before and After

To truly feel the power of the Memory Polisher blueprint, let's look at a live example of how a raw, disjointed thought dump is transformed when passed through your supervisor's guardrails.

The Raw Memory Dump (The "Before" Context)

Imagine typing or speaking this exact unedited stream of thoughts into your assistant:

"Let's see... my Uncle Puggie. He had this old workshop behind the barn on the farm. It always smelled like grease, old iron, and sweet cedar wood shavings. He had an ancient tractor - I think it was a 1952 model - and he would talk to it like it was an old mule. Every single Saturday morning, he'd try to turn that crank, and it would spit and splutter. He'd look at me, wink, and say, 'She's just clearing her throat, kiddo.' I want my grandkids to know how patient he was, and what that workshop felt like on a crisp morning."

The Polished Narrative Output (The "After" Result)

By applying our Memory Polisher blueprint, the assistant bypasses the temptation to create a cheesy, overly dramatic story and delivers a warm, clean record that preserves the true spirit of your recollection:

The Voice of the Workshop

My Uncle Puggie operated his world out of an old wood-frame workshop situated directly behind the main barn on the farm. To walk through that heavy wooden door was to step into a familiar sensory library. This space permanently smelled of dark machine grease, aged iron tools, and the sweet, clean scent of freshly cut cedar wood shavings.

At the center of his daily routines sat an ancient, faded tractor built in 1952. It was a temperamental machine, but Uncle Puggie never treated it with frustration; instead, he spoke to it with the quiet, steady patience one would show to an old farm mule. Every Saturday morning, I followed the exact same ritual. He would step up to the heavy iron crank, set his boots flat against the dirt, and give it a firm pull. The engine would invariably spit, splutter, and release a small cloud of gray smoke into the crisp air.

Without fail, Uncle Puggie would turn his head toward me, offer a slow wink, and say, "She's just clearing her throat, kiddo." That simple workshop taught me more about steady perseverance than any school lecture ever could. It is a memory anchored to the sound of sputtering iron, the warmth of a shared joke, and the beautiful, quiet patience of a man who knew exactly how to take his time.

Look at how the machine handled that text block. It didn't invent a fake background or make up characters. It simply took your raw, fragmented details. It arranged them with a gentle narrative rhythm, giving your family a beautiful vignette they can read and pass down for generations.

The Supervisor's Correction Guide

Every single time the AI returns a draft or a list of questions, remember that you are the primary historical supervisor. Think of this process as an interactive, conversational loop. If the machine adjusts a phrasing in a way that shifts the true meaning of your memory, you possess the absolute authority to fix it.

You do not have to settle for the first response the machine gives you. You can simply copy the text into your own notebook and change the words yourself, or type a direct correction back into the entry box. Let's look at how to guide your scribe back onto the right track:

If the AI sounds too dramatic: "That is a good start, but it sounds a bit too much like a movie trailer. Soften the adjectives and make it sound like a plain-spoken story told around a kitchen table."

If the AI guesses a detail incorrectly: "The story is accurate, but change the location from the front porch to the back kitchen garden, and remind the reader that it was raining that morning."

The technology is simply holding the digital pencil; the wisdom, truth, and ultimate authority belong entirely to you.

Mini-Milestone: Reflecting on Your Digital Legacy

Let's take a brief moment to celebrate the wonderful milestone you have reached in this chapter:

Rescued Memories: You learned how to use the Prompt Recipe to rescue raw, disjointed family memories from the intimidation of the blank page.

Protected Voice: You discovered how to set strict factual Constraints to prevent the machine from inventing details or altering your true voice.

Somatic Reset: You used a Heart-Opening Stretch to relieve physical tension in your posture while reflecting on your personal history.

Visual Order: You explored how to build a clean cataloging table to immediately bring systemized order to physical photo albums.

Take a moment to write a quick answer to this reflection prompt in your notebook:

What is one family story, ancestral name, or old photograph box that has been sitting in the back of my mind? How can I use a simple biographical prompt to safely explore its history today without worrying about perfection?

Moving Forward with Total Confidence

You are doing absolutely magnificent work. By bringing your extraordinary personal library of wisdom and life experience to the digital table, you have turned your virtual assistant into a deeply respectful, high-utility legacy partner that helps you share your stories entirely on your own terms. You are learning that prompting is a craft - one that becomes more natural every time you play with it.

Whenever you are ready, let's turn the page to Chapter 9, where we will enter a brand-new operational territory, learning how to use our assistant to tame household and financial clutter, simplify dense utility updates, and interpret warranty manuals without a single ounce of technical stress! Let's keep exploring!

Taming the Financial and Household Clutter

Open up your kitchen cabinet or take a glance at the paper drawer sitting near your telephone right now. For most of us, those hidden spaces contain a slow, constant buildup of modern household friction: home insurance updates, utility rate adjustments, medical benefit statements, and appliance user manuals printed in tiny, gray print. Today, we are going to bring your virtual assistant straight into the center of your kitchen to act as a clear-headed property coordinator.

Think about how much invisible energy we spend managing the modern household. Every month, your mailbox or computer inbox fills with dense, multi-page documents: home insurance policy updates, utility rate restructurings, medical explanation-of-benefits sheets, and lengthy appliance warranties packed with microscopic small print. You want to understand exactly how a new rule affects your budget, or what specific steps you need to take to protect a product investment. Still, you find yourself staring at a literal wall of legal and financial padding. Your eyes strain, your attention drifts, and your shoulders lock up as you think, "I just want a straight answer in plain English."

Traditional management guides treat household organization like a corporate bookkeeping job, piling on heavy spreadsheet formulas, complex filing software, and dense accounting terminology that feels like extra work.

Let's sweep that stressful approach off our table. Effective prompting is a learnable skill rather than a technical talent, and you do not need to be a corporate bookkeeper or a contract attorney to keep your household running beautifully. Your AI assistant is a brilliant, clear-headed administrative coordinator who loves reviewing technical text sheets. By feeding a dense policy update or an appliance manual into our trusted Prompt Recipe, you can instantly strip away the corporate filler, translate the confusing jargon into everyday speech, and build custom, scannable household tracking lists that keep you entirely in control of your castle. Think of it as a series of low-pressure experiments where small improvements matter far more than achieving immediate perfection.

The Recipe Ingredients for Clear Home Logistics

When we command AI to parse household or financial documents, the key to an independent, stress-free outcome lies entirely in our Context, Constraints, and Format bowls. We want to avoid sharing your true identity while still demanding absolute accuracy and a layout that is highly comfortable for your eyes.

Here is how we adjust our kitchen ingredients to conquer household clutter:

The Role: Give the AI a highly practical, precise, and plain-spoken administrative identity. This ensures the output reads like a direct briefing from a trusted household manager. For example: "Act as an expert, concise consumer advocate," or "Act as a meticulously organized household administrator."

The Context: Paste the raw text of a dense policy summary, warranty rule, or utility update here. Remember our sacred safety rule from Chapter 2: keep your private identity links out of the box entirely by using clear placeholders like [My Bank] or [My Utility Provider].

The Constraints: This is your vital financial quality control tool – your jargon-pruning guardrail. You explicitly command the machine: "Translate all complex legal and financial jargon into simple, everyday terms. Identify only the concrete action items, premium changes, or specific deadlines that affect the consumer, leaving out all repetitive corporate text. Do not invent any facts, policies, or figures."

The Format: Demand highly scannable, clean visual frameworks. Instead of dense paragraphs, command the tool to use numbered grids, bold highlights, or clean tables with explicit columns for action items and specific dates.

Reader Reviver Brain Break: The Wrist and Forearm Release

Before we open up our household management templates, let's check in with our hands and arms. When we look through household bills, organize filing cabinets, or type out logistical lists, our wrists and forearms build up significant, quiet, repetitive muscle tension that can restrict blood flow and cause upper-body strain.

Let's push back from the desktop for just sixty seconds to bring immediate, restorative flexibility back to your hands:

The Desk Release: Drop both of your hands completely away from your device or papers, letting your arms rest loosely in your lap. Take a deep, nose-inhale and a slow, mouth-exhale.

The Forward Stretch: Extend your right arm straight out in front of you at shoulder height, with your palm facing away from you. Your fingertips are pointing up toward the ceiling, as if you were pressing against an imaginary wall.

The Gentle Pull: Take your left hand, reach across, and gently pull the fingertips of your right hand back toward your body until you feel a clean, beautiful lengthening stretch along your inner wrist and forearm. Hold this gentle position for three slow, steady breaths.

The Counter Flip: Point the fingertips of your right hand down toward the floor, with your palm facing your body, and use your left hand to press the back of your hand gently toward you for another three counts.

Release your right arm, shake out your fingers completely, and repeat the exact same sequence with your left hand. Notice how quickly that small pause releases the deep ache in your wrists? This somatic exercise clears away physical fatigue, lowers your body's subtle stress response, and resets your concentration so you can manage your household projects with absolute calm.

Real-World Household Blueprints

Use these structured frameworks to instantly dissolve dense fine print and bring total clarity to your home administration. You can copy these precise layouts directly into your assistant today:

Blueprint 1: The Policy Simplifier

Use this framework to strip away the legal padding from insurance policies, rate adjustments, or service notices.

Role: Act as an expert, plain-English consumer advocate, and policy analyst.

Goal: Review the attached dense household policy update and extract the essential changes affecting the customer.

Context: [Paste the text of your household insurance update or utility rate sheet here, leaving personal names blank].

Constraints: Strip out all repetitive legal disclosures and corporate padding. Translate all technical jargon into simple everyday language. Do not create any outside context or add unverified assumptions.

Format: Present the final answer as a single-sentence headline showing the biggest change, followed by a brief numbered list of specific cost adjustments, rule updates, or deadlines.

Blueprint 2: The Home Asset Cataloger

Use this framework to build an organized record of your home valuables for your physical files or insurance records.

Role: Act as a meticulously organized household administrator.

Goal: Create a clean, structural tracking table to help me build a comprehensive household asset inventory for my insurance records.

Context: I want to document the major appliances, electronics, and valuable items, room by room, throughout my home, so I can store the details safely in my physical file cabinet.

Constraints: Keep the column names practical, simple, and entirely scannable for easy manual entry. Avoid complex digital database jargon.

Format: Organize the final response into a clean table with separate columns for 'Room Location', 'Item Description', 'Brand/Model Number', 'Approximate Purchase Year', and 'Estimated Replacement Cost'.

Blueprint 3: The Warranty Breakdown

Use this framework to instantly find maintenance guidelines or hidden return deadlines inside product user manuals.

Role: Act as a practical, concise technical assistant.

Goal: Review the attached appliance manual and extract the essential maintenance steps and return policies.

Context: [Paste the text of a new product warranty or instruction leaflet here].

Constraints: Remove all promotional sales text and unnecessary engineering definitions. Keep the instructions under four sentences per category.

Format: Present the final answer in two short, distinct bulleted lists: one labeled 'Required Maintenance Steps' and the other labeled 'Warranty Rules and Deadlines'.

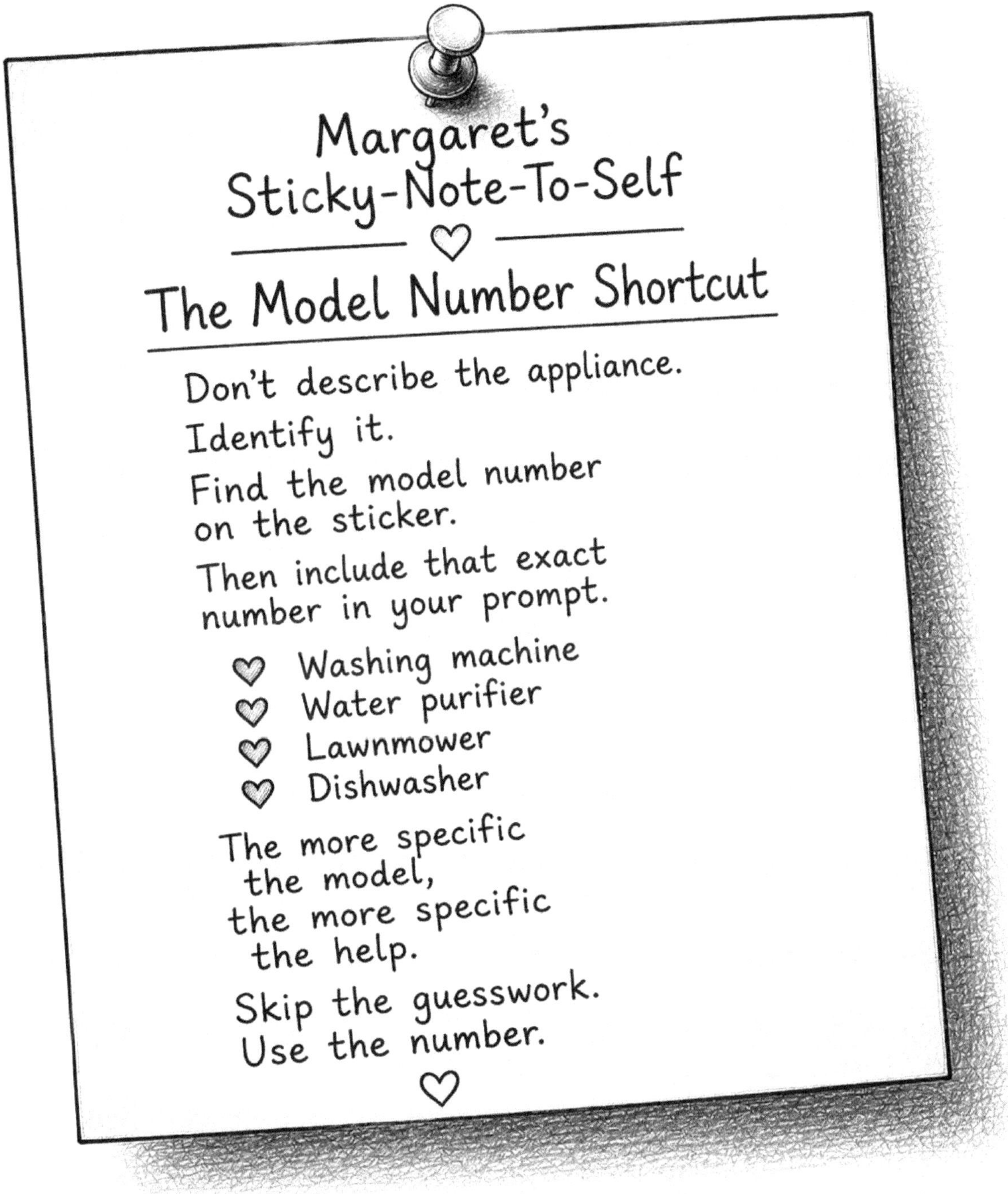

When you are looking for help with a specific household item - like a flashing error code on a washing machine, a filter replacement schedule for a water purifier, or a warranty timeline for a lawnmower - you don't have to worry about typing out long descriptions. Every modern appliance has a small silver or white sticker hidden somewhere on its frame (usually inside a door lip, on the back panel, or underneath the base) containing a string of letters and numbers known as the **Model Number**.

Instead of searching the internet through a maze of advertisements, simply type that exact model number directly into your Context bowl alongside your recipe. Your assistant can instantly anchor its pattern-matcher to that specific piece of machinery, giving you exact, customized household steps without a single ounce of guesswork.

The Recipe in Action: Before and After

To truly feel the power of the Policy Simplifier blueprint, let's look at a live example of how a dense wall of corporate communication is stripped of its noise and converted into a clear briefing.

The Raw Document (The "Before" Context)

Imagine receiving a letter from your local provider and pasting this dense block into the prompt box:

"Pursuant to the regulatory updates mandated by the regional commission under statute 402-B, notice is hereby given that, effective July 1st, a tier-structured operational cost adjustment will be integrated into the standard baseline utility tariff. Customers utilizing standard residential connections will observe an increase in the peak-hour kw/h volumetric pricing index from $0.14 to $0.16. Furthermore, please be advised that the mandatory grace period for online balance reconciliation has been amended. To avoid the administrative late fee penalty ($15.00), balances must be cleared within fourteen (14) business days of invoice issuance, rather than the previous twenty-one (21) day cycle. Failure to comply with the updated payment structures may trigger automated notifications."

The Plain-English Output (The "After" Result)

By applying our Policy Simplifier blueprint, your assistant cuts straight through the intimidating language and drops this clear summary onto your digital desk:

Headline: Starting July 1st, your electricity rates will increase during peak hours, and you will have one less week to pay your monthly bill.

Price Change: Your peak-hour electric rate is rising from **$0.14 to $0.16** per kilowatt-hour.

New Deadline: You must pay your bill within **14 business days** of receiving it, instead of the old 21-day timeline.

Late Penalty: Payments made after the 14-day mark will trigger an automatic **$15.00 late fee**.

Look at that screen. The machine stripped away 30 words of legal disclosures and regulatory statutes, leaving behind only the hard facts that actually affect your checkbook and calendar. You can write those dates directly into your kitchen planner with total confidence.

The Conversational Correction Loop

Every time the assistant delivers a breakdown or formats an asset list, remember that your life experience remains the final anchor. If the AI condenses a policy clause in a way that feels a bit unclear, or if it skips over a detail you care about, you are always the supervisor in charge.

You never have to accept a confusing response. Think of your prompting as a normal, back-and-forth conversation with an administrative assistant. You can use your authority to refine the output using direct corrections right in the chat window:

If the explanation is still too technical: "Explain that second premium point again using a simple analogy to car insurance, so it is completely plain."

If you want to look up a specific machine: "Here is the model number for my hot water heater: [Insert Model Number]. Look through the maintenance text I pasted above and tell me exactly how often I need to flush the tank according to the manufacturer."

The machine provides the processing power, but your common sense directs the outcome.

Mini-Milestone: Reflecting on Your Operational Order

Let's pause and note the powerful structural control you have brought into your space during this short chapter:

Jargon Stripping: You learned how to use the Prompt Recipe to effortlessly strip out legal filler and corporate jargon from household paperwork.

Asset Mapping: You discovered how to use the Format ingredient to command the AI to build clean, custom asset charts for your physical records.

Physical Release: You used a Wrist and Forearm Release to physically relieve arm and finger muscle tension away from the desk.

Privacy Guardrails: You practiced using anonymized placeholders to review real-world documents with total privacy and peace of mind.

Take a brief moment to write down your response to this reflection prompt in your notebook:

What is one dense home manual, utility change notice, or insurance policy update that has been sitting on my kitchen counter, causing me a hint of overthinking? How can I safely test it in the prompt box today using placeholders?

Moving Forward with Total Confidence

You are doing absolutely magnificent work. By matching your deep, lifelong practical wisdom with clear, structured instructions, you have turned your virtual assistant into a highly responsive household manager that helps you keep your affairs in pristine order entirely on your own terms. You are building momentum with every single page.

You have successfully taken the heavy administrative weight of home management and handed it to an automated engine that handles it in seconds. Your affairs are in pristine order entirely under your supervision. Close the laptop screen down, take a long, well-deserved break away from the desk, and let your body unwind completely before we connect this digital logic directly back to physical, outdoor exploration.

Cultivating Hobbies, Gardening, and Earth-Based Craftsmanship

There is a profound, comforting beauty in working with your hands – the crisp snap of a homemade sourdough crust cooling on the counter, the smell of sweet cedar wood shavings on a workbench, or the feel of rich, damp soil as you tuck a heritage tomato seedling into a backyard garden bed. Today, we are taking our digital tools completely out of the office and bringing them directly onto the soil and into the workshop to enrich your lifelong, hands-on pastimes.

Today, we are shifting our focus to the things that truly bring warmth and fulfillment to your week. We are going to look at how to use your assistant to enrich your hands-on hobbies - whether you want to plan a seasonal vegetable garden, troubleshoot an heirloom sourdough baking project, adjust a favorite knitting pattern, or map out the assembly steps for a weekend woodworking craft.

Think about how easy it is to hit a creative block when pursuing a lifelong hobby. Perhaps you want to plant a small patch of heirloom tomatoes and herbs. Still, you are confused about companion planting or how to handle local pests without harsh chemicals. Maybe you want to bake a fresh loaf of traditional crusty bread, but your kitchen temperature has changed with the seasons and your sourdough starter isn't rising properly. Or perhaps you have found a beautiful quilting pattern. The problem is that the measurements are listed for a king-sized mattress, and you want to scale it down perfectly for a grandchild's crib.

Traditional internet searches stifle these creative pastimes. When you look up a simple gardening or crafting question online, you are immediately buried under an avalanche of chaotic forums, conflicting advice columns, and flashing retail advertisements trying to sell you expensive tools you don't even need.

Let's clear that noisy clutter off our table entirely. Effective prompting is a learnable skill rather than a technical talent, and you do not need to be a professional botanist or a master artisan to bring your creative projects to life. Your AI assistant is a highly resourceful, patient study partner that has instant access to millions of traditional manual guides, historical gardening records, and classic crafting patterns. Think of this as a series of low-pressure experiments where small improvements matter far more than achieving immediate perfection. By feeding your unique, hands-on goals into our trusted Prompt Recipe, you can bypass the marketing noise and extract clean, hyper-local gardening matrices, step-by-step baking fixes, and perfectly scaled crafting checklists that honor your time and intelligence.

The Recipe Ingredients for Physical Craftsmanship

When we ask AI to act as a companion for our hobbies and crafts, our Prompt Recipe adjusts to emphasize hyper-local precision, practical tools, and clear structural order. We want to avoid vague, general tips; instead, we want the machine to provide concrete, actionable blueprints tailored to our regional climate, kitchen setup, or materials list. Think of this process as a collaborative, low-pressure experiment where you maintain full creative control.

To unlock a high-utility result, we focus on specific bowls of our recipe layout:

The Role: Give the AI a highly specialized, practical, and encouraging artisan mindset. This ensures the voice sounds like a seasoned old-school mentor sharing wisdom over a potting bench or a workbench. For example: "Act as a master organic gardener and local horticultural expert," or "Act as an encouraging heirloom baking instructor."

The Context: Describe the exact parameters of your project. Don't hold back the details - list your exact geographic climate or zip code, the orientation of your garden beds, your experience level, or the specific yarn, fabric, and wood dimensions you already have on hand.

The Constraints: Set strict boundaries to filter out expensive commercial products, complicated high-tech gadgets, or overwhelming jargon - your natural craftsmanship guardrail. You can explicitly command the tool: "Focus entirely on low-cost, natural methods and simple hand tools. Avoid suggesting complex technical systems or commercial chemical fertilizers. Do not invent any historical horticultural parameters or unverified guidelines."

The Format: Direct the assistant to provide highly scannable, visual arrangements you can print or take straight into the garden or kitchen. Demand clean bulleted lists, bold instructional steps, or structural grids with columns for planting dates, care steps, and tool lists.

Reader Reviver Brain Break: The Seated Torso Twist Reboot

Before we open up our creative hobby blueprints, let’s check in with our backs and core. Focusing intently on a digital layout or spending long hours hunched over a sewing table, potting bench, or kitchen counter can compress our lower spine, freezing our posture and limiting deep, creative blood flow.

Let's push back from the desktop for just sixty seconds to bring a beautiful sense of alignment and spaciousness back to your torso:

The Planted Base: Sit comfortably upright and tall in your chair, letting your hands rest loosely on your knees. Plant both of your feet completely flat on the floor, feeling the stable, solid connection of the ground beneath you.

The Spinal Lift: Inhale deeply through your nose for a count of four, imagining a soft string gently lifting the top of your head up toward the ceiling to elongate your spine and drop your shoulders away from your ears.

The Rightward Glide: As you exhale softly through your mouth for a count of four, gently twist your upper body to the right. Place your left hand on the outside of your right thigh, and let your right hand rest on the back or side of your chair seat. Cast your gaze comfortably over your right shoulder.

The Center Pause: Hold this gentle twist for three slow, steady breaths, feeling your lower back and ribs expand wide. Slowly unwind back to the center on a calm inhale.

The Counter Sweep: Exhale and repeat the sequence on the left side, placing your right hand on your left thigh and comfortably looking over your left shoulder for another three breaths. Return smoothly to the center.

Let out a long, clearing sigh and let your arms hang loosely by your sides. Notice how that small physical movement releases the dull ache in your lower back? This simple somatic reset stretches your paraspinal muscles, opens up your diaphragm for deep breathing, and entirely clears the mental fog so you can approach your creative hobbies with calm, rooted independence.

Real-World Craftsmanship Blueprints

Use these functional frameworks to instantly translate your creative curiosity into practical, real-world success. You can copy these precise layouts directly into your assistant today:

Blueprint 1: The Companion Planting Grid

Use this framework to align your backyard soil with nature's natural partnerships, using our established table format to protect your visual focus.

Role: Act as a master organic gardener and local horticultural expert.

Goal: Create a custom seasonal companion planting guide for a small backyard vegetable garden.

Context: I am planting three raised beds in [Insert Your Town/State or Zip Code] and want to grow heirloom tomatoes, sweet bell peppers, and bush beans. I want to naturally repel common garden pests and maximize my space.

Constraints: Focus strictly on natural, organic methods and simple companion herbs or flowers. Do not suggest commercial chemical sprays or complex automated irrigation setups.

Format: Organize the final response into a clean table with columns for 'Main Vegetable', 'Best Companion Plants', 'Plants to Avoid Nearby', and 'Natural Pest Protection Tips'.

Blueprint 2: The Kitchen Troubleshooter

Use this framework to rescue an heirloom culinary project when environmental variables change with the seasons.

Role: Act as a patient, encouraging master baker and heirloom culinary instructor.

Goal: Diagnose a specific sourdough baking problem and provide a clear, step-by-step correction plan.

Context: I am baking a traditional wild-yeast sourdough loaf with a mature starter, but my recent loaves are turning out dense and heavy, with a flat, gummy crumb rather than an airy, light texture. My kitchen is currently cool, around 65 degrees Fahrenheit.

Constraints: Explain the solution using simple kitchen analogies, keeping each step to 4 sentences or fewer. Do not use overly technical food-science jargon.

Format: Present the final answer as a brief explanation of why this happened, followed by a clean, numbered list of three practical adjustments I can make to my proofing or timing today.

Blueprint 3: The Pattern Scaling Assistant

Use this framework to handle the transparent mathematical translations required to scale personal craft layouts perfectly.

Role: Act as a meticulous, encouraging sewing and quilting mentor.

Goal: Translate and scale down a complex layout calculation into a clear, beginner-friendly step breakdown.

Context: I want to adapt a traditional quilt block pattern originally sized for a standard queen bed and scale it down to create a warm baby blanket measuring 36 inches by 36 inches. I have basic cotton fabric cuts available.

Constraints: Keep the math completely transparent and straightforward, avoiding any confusing manufacturing abbreviations or industrial codes.

Format: Present the final instructions in a clean, scannable format, featuring a single bold headline that shows the exact cutting dimensions, followed by a short bulleted list of step-by-step assembly instructions.

When you use your assistant to build a seasonal planting schedule, prune backyard fruit trees, or source cover crops for your garden soil, remember to always tuck your exact **Zip Code** or local town into the Context bowl. Plant growth relies entirely on local microclimates and frost cycles. By sharing your regional location, you instantly signal the assistant's pattern-matcher to filter out irrelevant international growing schedules, giving you precise calendar boundaries that match the actual earth outside your kitchen window.

The Recipe in Action: Before and After

To see how the Kitchen Troubleshooter blueprint instantly tames confusing baking variables, let's observe a live comparison of how a frustrating, cool-weather sourdough mishap is broken down into simple, common-sense kitchen adjustments.

The Raw Problem (The "Before" Context)

Imagine typing this raw, disappointed thought dump into the text box after a morning in a cold kitchen:

"My starter usually bubbles like crazy, but today it's just sitting there sluggish because it's winter and the kitchen is freezing. My loaf didn't rise at all in the oven; it looks like a flat brick, and the inside is sticky like glue. I don't want to use commercial yeast, I just want to know how to fix my dough timing using what I have."

The Plain-English Solution (The "After" Result)

By applying our specialized culinary blueprint, your assistant avoids overwhelming you with scientific biological data and hands you a clear, comforting explanation alongside three simple action steps:

Why This Happened: Sourdough is a living culture that slows down dramatically when the ambient temperature drops. In a 65-degree kitchen, the wild yeast takes nearly twice as long to ferment, meaning your dough went into the oven "under-proofed," resulting in a heavy, flat, and gummy texture.

Create a Warm Microclimate: For your next bake, place your jar of starter inside your turned-off kitchen oven, with only the internal oven light on. This small bulb generates a gentle, draft-free warmth that brings the ambient temperature inside up to a cozy 75 degrees.

Extend the Bulk Rise: Do not rush the clock based on standard summer recipes. Allow your mixed dough to rest on the counter for an extra two to three hours, watching for the volume to visibly expand by roughly half before shaping.

The Visual Poke Test: Before baking, gently press your floured fingertip into the dough about half an inch. If the indentation springs back instantly, it needs more time; if it springs back slowly and leaves a slight dent, it is perfectly proofed and ready for the hot oven.

Look at how clear that layout is. The machine completely bypassed industrial food-science jargon, delivering plain-spoken home guidance that keeps you completely independent and successful at your own countertop.

The Supervisor's Sovereignty Guardrail

Every single time the AI fills out a planting chart, breaks down a pattern calculation, or suggests a baking timeline, remember that your own common sense and life experience remain the ultimate authority. Think of this process as an interactive, conversational loop with a digital apprentice. If the tool suggests an outdoor planting date that feels far too early for your local frost history, or recommends a wood cut that doesn't feel right for your materials, trust your gut and overrule the computer!

You possess the absolute authority to adjust the directions. You can step in as the final supervisor right in the conversation box by guiding the assistant back onto the path:

To correct a frost line: "Our spring ground stays frozen until late April, and we always get a late frost. Adjust the entire heirloom tomato planting schedule to account for this regional restriction so I don't lose my seedlings."

To change a material dimension: "That woodworking step is clear, but I am working with a 1-inch thick cedar plank rather than a standard pine board. Recalculate the pocket hole depths based strictly on this adjustment."

The machine holds the historical database, but you are always the supervisor standing on the actual soil.

Mini-Milestone: Reflecting on Your Hands-On Potential

Let's pause and note the wonderful layer of creative freedom you have brought into your space during this short chapter:

Artisan Mentorship: You learned how to use the Prompt Recipe to turn your assistant into an encouraging, low-pressure artisan mentor.

Marketing Filter: You discovered how setting strict natural Constraints filters out expensive marketing gimmicks and commercial chemical solutions.

Somatic Realignment: You used a Seated Torso Twist to physically relieve spinal compression and open up your deep lateral thinking away from the monitor.

Hyper-Local Design: You practiced applying local context to unlock custom, step-by-step blueprints for gardening, baking, and hand-crafts.

Take a brief moment to jot down a quick answer to this reflection prompt in your notebook:

What is one hands-on project, backyard garden bed, or traditional kitchen skill that I have been wanting to explore or refine? How can

I use a simple companion role prompt to safely unlock a fresh entry point into it this week without worrying about immediate perfection?

Moving Forward with Total Confidence

You are doing absolutely magnificent work. By matching your rich library of practical life experience with clear structural instructions, you have transformed your virtual assistant into a deeply respectful, high-utility craftsmanship partner that expands your creative freedom entirely on your own terms. You are treating the tool as a helpful peer, building incredible momentum with every action.

Prompting is not a technical talent; it is an active craft that becomes more natural every single time you apply it to the physical world you love. Trust your instincts over the computer chips every single time. Stand up, stretch your torso out fully, and let your creative energy recharge before we bring these skills into the local public organizations that rely on your leadership.

Becoming the Community Coordinator

The absolute cultural and logistical backbone of our towns does not sit inside corporate high-rises – it is found around local volunteer tables, historical society meetings, and community fundraisers.

Many mature creators serve as the vital framework for these groups, yet that incredible gift of service often comes with a steep price in tedious paperwork. Today, we are lifting your digital autonomy off your private desk and bringing its processing power directly into the community organizations you lead.

Think about the incredible gift of your time.

Many adults over fifty serve as the absolute cultural and logistical backbone of our local communities: chairing historical societies, coordinating church fundraisers, running neighborhood watch associations, or organizing busy community garden plots. Yet the reward of volunteering often comes with a steep price in time and energy. You sit down to organize an upcoming potluck or write a donation request, and suddenly, you are buried under hours of paperwork. You find yourself struggling to arrange meeting notes into formal minutes, or trying to format an attractive announcement flyer that stands out on a local bulletin board without looking corporate or clinical.

Traditional group management systems tell you to adopt heavy, complex project coordination software, learn confusing digital calendar links, or download corporate text programs that turn a heartfelt local effort into an overwhelming second career.

Let's sweep that administrative friction off our table.

Effective prompting is a learnable skill rather than a technical talent, and you do not need to be a corporate secretary or a public relations expert to lead your local group beautifully. Your AI assistant functions as an exceptionally diligent, highly efficient committee assistant who stands ready to hold the digital pencil for you. Think of this as an ongoing series of low-pressure experiments where small improvements matter far more than achieving immediate perfection. By feeding your raw, hand-scrawled notes or upcoming event ideas into our trusted Prompt Recipe, you can instantly generate warm, diplomatic outreach letters, beautifully structured meeting minutes, and crisp, engaging neighborhood announcements that respect your intelligence, save your hours, and leave you entirely free to focus on the human connections that make community life so deeply rewarding.

The Recipe Ingredients for Diplomatic Outreach

When we deploy AI to help manage community organizations and public communication, our ingredients shift to emphasize a warm, inclusive neighborhood tone, precise action deadlines, and highly scannable formatting. We want to avoid aggressive, cold business language and ensure that every announcement sounds like a thoughtful, mature resident speaking directly to neighbors across a front gate. Think of this process as a collaborative, low-pressure experiment where you maintain full creative control.

To ensure your community communications land beautifully on the very first try, we focus on these specific ingredients:

The Role: Give the AI a warm, community-minded, and highly diplomatic administrative identity. This guides the voice to maintain a balanced, welcoming posture that builds goodwill across a group. For example: "Act as a warm, inclusive neighborhood association secretary," or "Act as a diplomatic community organizer and volunteer coordinator."

The Context: This is where you dump your raw, unorganized thoughts or hurried meeting scribbles. Don't worry about punctuation or order here – simply type out the date of the next gathering, what items people should bring to the potluck, who spoke at the meeting, and what decisions were reached.

The Constraints: Set firm quality-control guardrails to prevent your text from sounding like a dry corporate form letter or an aggressive sales pitch – your diplomatic outreach guardrail. You can explicitly command the tool: "Keep the language completely warm, inviting, and neighborly. Avoid cold corporate buzzwords and ensure all action dates or deadlines are clearly highlighted for easy reading. Do not invent any outside community rules or historical project parameters."

The Format: Direct the assistant to build highly scannable visual structures. For meeting updates, use the layout command to generate clear tables with separate columns for decisions and action tasks. For announcements, demand crisp bullet points with plenty of clean white space to prevent eye strain.

Reader Reviver Brain Break: The Vocal and Jaw Release

Before we look at our ready-to-use community blueprints, let's check in with our face, jaw, and breathing. Leading public events, coordinating with large groups, or focusing intently on writing public flyers can cause us to unconsciously clamp our teeth together and hold stress in our facial muscles, triggering shallow breathing and tightening our upper neck.

Let's push back from the keyboard for just sixty seconds to completely unlock your facial muscles and invite deep, spacious calm into your body:

The Hands-Free Base: Sit comfortably tall in your chair, letting your hands drop completely off your device to rest palms-up in your lap. Let your feet settle flat on the floor beneath you, anchoring your stance.

The Jaw Drop: Inhale slowly through your nose for a count of four. As you exhale softly through your mouth, completely open your mouth wide, letting your lower jaw drop down as far as it can comfortably go, as if you were expressing total surprise. Hold it open for three seconds.

The Cheek Glide: Move your jaw gently from side to side two times while it is open, letting the large masseter muscles on the sides of your face completely soften and release their grip.

The Sweeping Hum: Close your lips loosely, leaving your teeth slightly separated inside. Take a long, deep breath into your stomach for a count of four, and as you exhale, let out a soft, low, rolling humming sound. Feel the gentle physical vibration loosen the tissue around your throat, lips, and forehead.

Let your face go completely loose and take a normal, easy breath. Notice how that brief physical break clears away the tight, heavy mask of fatigue around your eyes and forehead? This simple somatic reset lowers your nervous system's subtle tension loop, clears your working memory, and restores a grounded, calm clarity so you can step into your community spaces with authentic confidence.

Real-World Community Blueprints

Use these structured frameworks to instantly dissolve the administrative headache of public volunteering and keep your local organization running beautifully. You can copy these precise layouts directly into your assistant today:

Blueprint 1: The Event Flyer Blueprint

Use this framework to generate an engaging, welcoming public announcement flyer for an upcoming community gathering.

Role: Act as a warm, inclusive neighborhood association secretary and event designer.

Goal: Generate an engaging, welcoming public announcement flyer for an upcoming community gathering.

Context: Our local historical society is hosting an autumn charity potluck and guest speaker event on Saturday, October 17th, at 4:00 PM in the community center basement. The speaker is a local historian discussing early town landmarks. Residents should bring a side dish or dessert, and all donations go toward repairing the historical park gate.

Constraints: Keep the tone entirely friendly, warm, and inviting. Do not use corporate event jargon. Ensure the entry cost and donation details look definitive and clear.

Format: Present this as a crisp, printable announcement layout with a bold headline, followed by a scannable bulleted list showing the exact 'When', 'Where', and 'What to Bring' details, ending with a short call-to-action note.

Blueprint 2: The Minutes Restructurer

Use this framework to systematically format a messy block of raw meeting notes using our established column tracking layout.

Role: Act as a meticulously organized, concise committee assistant.

Goal: Transform a messy block of raw, hurried meeting notes into an organized, professional summary of minutes.

Context: [Paste or type your raw, hurried notes from your recent volunteer or club meeting here, including names and basic tasks discussed].

Constraints: Strip out all conversational filler, off-topic side remarks, and repetitive text. Keep all summaries objective and completely plain-spoken.

Format: Organize the final response into a clean, easy-to-read table with separate columns for 'Topic Discussed', 'Core Decision Reached', 'Assigned Volunteer Name', and 'Action Deadline'.

Blueprint 3: The Diplomatic Outreach Letter

Use this framework to translate a fundraising goal or project invitation into an exceptionally respectful, balanced letter.

Role: Act as a polite, firm, and highly diplomatic community coordinator.

Goal: Write a short, courteous letter to a local business owner requesting a donation or inviting them to support a community project.

Context: I am writing on behalf of our local community garden committee to invite Mr. Davis, the owner of the hometown hardware store, to donate three bags of fertilizer or sponsor a tool shed. Express our deep gratitude for his long-standing business presence in our area.

Constraints: Keep the entire message to two paragraphs or fewer. Ensure the tone is exceptionally respectful yet definitive, avoiding pushy sales rhetoric or overly complex corporate contract language.

Format: Present the response as a clean, ready-to-copy letter draft with clear placeholders for dates and contact lines.

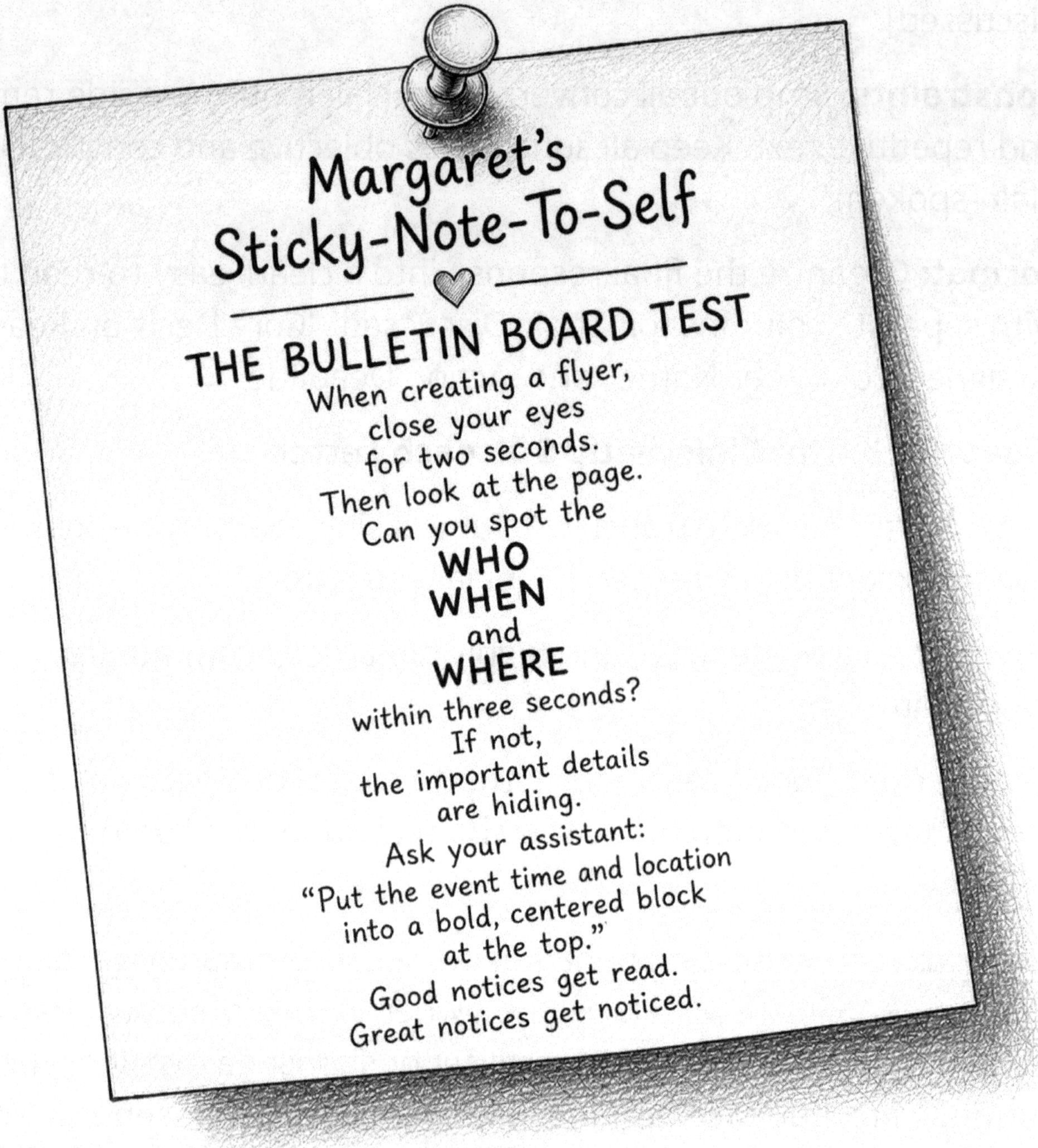

When your assistant generates a printable flyer layout or a public group email announcement, review the text on your screen and apply a quick visual check called the Bulletin Board Test: close your eyes for 2 seconds, then open them and look at the page. Is the absolute main point – the Who, When, and Where – visible in bold within the first three seconds? If the vital details are buried deep inside long sentences, tell your assistant: "Put the event time and location into a bold, centered block at the top so it is impossible to miss on a crowded wall."

The Recipe in Action: Before and After

To see how the Minutes Restructurer blueprint instantly clears away group administrative clutter, let's look at a live example: a chaotic, hurried jumble of notes taken during a lively community meeting is distilled into an orderly, professional tracking layout.

The Raw Notes (The "Before" Context)

Imagine pasting these frantic, hand-written meeting scribbles straight into your prompt box:

"Okay, so the meeting started late because the key to the room was missing. Sarah said the historical society bank account has $412 left.

We spent way too long talking about the broken fence – Bob thinks it was a runaway truck, but Martha says it's just old age. Anyway, we decided we have to fix it before the winter frost. Bob said he'd call a local contractor by next Friday to get a solid quote. Then we talked about the upcoming bake sale. Mary agreed to handle the flyer designs and get them printed by October 1st. Joe complained about the parking lot lights again, but we ran out of time and said we'd look into it next month."

The Organized Output (The "After" Result)

By processing these notes through your committee assistant persona, the machine strips out the side debates and hands you a clean, scannable table ready for distribution:

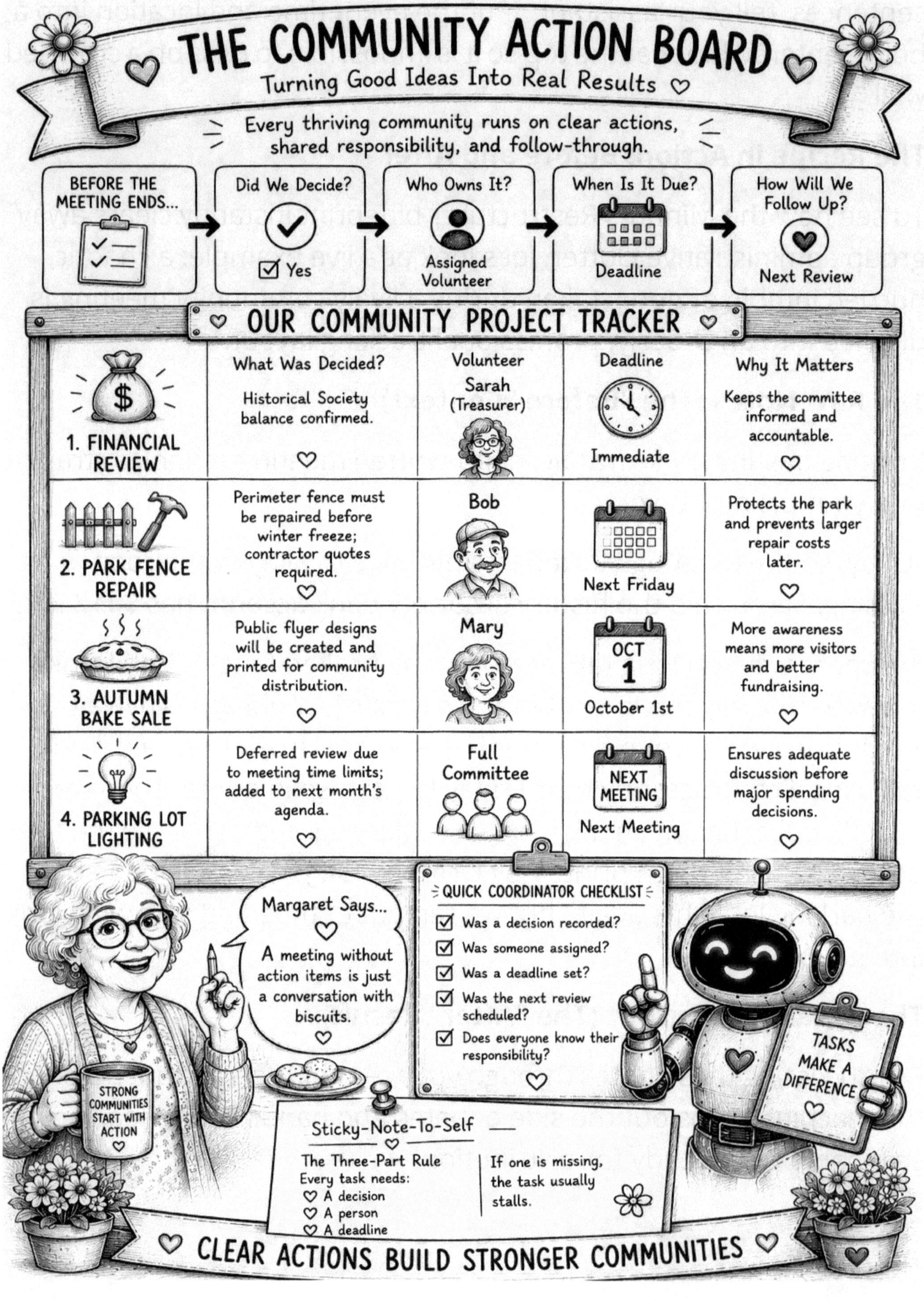
THE COMMUNITY ACTION BOARD
Turning Good Ideas Into Real Results
Every thriving community runs on clear actions, shared responsibility, and follow-through.
BEFORE THE MEETING ENDS...
Did We Decide?
Yes
Who Owns It?
Assigned Volunteer
When Is It Due?
Deadline
How Will We Follow Up?
Next Review
OUR COMMUNITY PROJECT TRACKER
What Was Decided?
Volunteer
Deadline
Why It Matters
1. FINANCIAL REVIEW
Historical Society balance confirmed.
Sarah (Treasurer)
Immediate
Keeps the committee informed and accountable.
2. PARK FENCE REPAIR
Perimeter fence must be repaired before winter freeze; contractor quotes required.
Bob
Next Friday
Protects the park and prevents larger repair costs later.
3. AUTUMN BAKE SALE
Public flyer designs will be created and printed for community distribution.
Mary
OCT 1
October 1st
More awareness means more visitors and better fundraising.
4. PARKING LOT LIGHTING
Deferred review due to meeting time limits; added to next month's agenda.
Full Committee
NEXT MEETING
Next Meeting
Ensures adequate discussion before major spending decisions.
Margaret Says...
A meeting without action items is just a conversation with biscuits.
QUICK COORDINATOR CHECKLIST
Was a decision recorded?
Was someone assigned?
Was a deadline set?
Was the next review scheduled?
Does everyone know their responsibility?
TASKS MAKE A DIFFERENCE
STRONG COMMUNITIES START WITH ACTION
Sticky-Note-To-Self
The Three-Part Rule
Every task needs:
A decision
A person
A deadline
If one is missing, the task usually stalls.
CLEAR ACTIONS BUILD STRONGER COMMUNITIES

Look at how beautifully that hits your eyes.

The assistant bypassed the twenty-minute argument about the runaway truck and the missing room key, focusing strictly on the actionable entries your volunteers need to see to remain organized and independent.

The Supervisor's Communal Sovereignty

Every time your assistant organizes a set of minutes or polishes an outreach letter, remember that your human experience remains the ultimate supervisor.

Think of this process as an interactive, conversational loop with a digital apprentice.

If the machine suggests a phrase that feels a little too formal or doesn't match the unique, warm personality of your town's neighborhood club, you hold the absolute authority to rewrite it!

You do not have to settle for a generic form letter. You can step in as the final supervisor right in the conversation box by guiding the assistant back onto the proper path:

To soften an outreach tone: "Make the letter to Mr. Davis sound slightly more casual and warm, as we have known him for years, and he always supports our local schools. Keep it respectful but neighborly."

To correct an error in a set of minutes: "The table is beautifully organized, but swap the assignments for the bake sale and the fence repair. Mary is handling the contractor quotes, and Bob is looking after the flyers."

The technology provides the processing power, but your wisdom ensures the communication remains authentically human.

Mini-Milestone: Reflecting on Your Community Coordination

Let's pause and note the wonderful milestones of public leadership and independence you have added to your notebook in this chapter:

Flyer Autonomy: You learned how to use the Prompt Recipe to completely remove the heavy, time-consuming burden of writing public event announcements.

Jargon Filtering: You discovered how to use strict neighborly Constraints to filter out stiff corporate jargon in favor of a warm, inclusive group tone.

Physical Reset: You used a Vocal and Jaw Release to physically dissolve facial muscle tension and ground your short-term focus away from the desk.

Structured Records: You explored how to use clean visual tables to turn a chaotic block of meeting notes into beautifully organized, structurally sound records.

Take a brief moment to write down your response to this reflection prompt in your notebook:

What is one upcoming volunteer task, civic club meeting, or neighborhood gathering that has been sitting on my calendar or drawing on my free time? How can I use a clean coordinator recipe to streamline its administration today without overthinking the text?

Moving Forward with Total Confidence

You are doing absolutely magnificent work. By combining your deep library of practical life experience, common sense, and personal relationships with clear structural inputs, you have turned your virtual assistant into a highly responsive, high-utility community asset that serves your leadership entirely on your own terms. You are leaning into your capability, step by easy step.

Now that our Phase 2 practical application chapters are beautifully complete, unified, and whole, let's turn the page to Chapter 12, where we will enter Phase 3 of our journey together, unlocking our single, comprehensive troubleshooting playbook to master system gaps, clear away platform differences, and secure permanent digital independence! Let's keep exploring!

BONUS - The Standalone Troubleshooting Toolkit

Pouring the final drop of coffee into our cups, take a look out the window and notice how much the scenery has changed since we first sat down together. Pull your chair in close, take a long, slow sip of your coffee, and let's settle into our final chapter together. Relax your face, unclench your jaw, and feel the solid grounding of the floor beneath your feet. We have arrived at Phase 3 of our journey.

You have already broken the ice with your digital assistant, safely secured your privacy guardrails, mastered the core engine of the Prompt Recipe, and successfully deployed it to conquer daily writing, organizing, and brainstorming tasks.

Today, we are going to build your ultimate layer of digital independence: your troubleshooting playbook.

Think about the last time you tried to learn a new piece of technology or software. Everything goes beautifully as long as you are following a perfect script. But the moment you click a button and an unexpected screen pops up, or the moment the machine gives you a response that doesn't make any sense, everything grinds to a halt. You freeze, a familiar wave of tech anxiety creeps back into your shoulders, and you feel defeated.

Traditional software manuals scatter little warning boxes and dense error codes across every single page, creating a digital minefield. They treat every unexpected result like a critical system failure, using flashing red symbols and cold codes that offer no guidance on how to move forward.

Let's clear all that messiness away. Effective prompting is a learnable skill rather than a technical talent, and you do not need to be a computer engineer to handle an unhelpful digital output.

We have gathered every common digital hiccup, every strange AI quirk, and every minor platform difference into this one single, standalone home. Think of this final module as a low-pressure training ground where small, curious adjustments matter far more than achieving immediate perfection.

When the AI gives you a strange, vague, or incorrect response, it is never a reflection of your intelligence, and you haven't broken the system. It is simply a sign that the machine's pattern-matching engine hit a temporary gap. It ran into a patch of fog because the phrasing wasn't quite specific enough to chart a clear path. You are the supervisor in charge, and with three simple verbal tools, you can steer your assistant back on track in seconds while maintaining complete creative control.

The Three Common AI Quirks (and How to Fix Them)

When a prompt doesn't land perfectly on the first try, it usually falls into one of three predictable patterns. Here is exactly what is happening under the hood and the simple phrases you can type to correct it instantly:

1. The Output is Far Too Vague or Generic

What it looks like: You ask for dinner ideas or a travel itinerary, and the AI gives you an incredibly boring, generic response that reads like a textbook entry or an old encyclopedia.

Why it happens: The machine didn't receive enough Constraints or Context in your recipe, so it defaulted to the safest, most common average answers in its database.

The technical fix: Do not start a new page or clear your slate. Simply type this phrase right into the existing box:

"That is a bit too generic. Please rewrite this focusing heavily on unique, hands-on details and apply these specific constraints: [Insert a new rule, e.g., 'No seafood' or 'Keep it under three sentences']."

2. The Assistant is Sounding Like a Sterile Robot

What it looks like: You ask the AI to help polish an email to a friend or a contractor, and it delivers a stiff, overly formal message packed with heavy corporate jargon like "Please find attached herewith" or "Per my previous correspondence."

Why it happens: The machine temporarily dropped its assigned Role or the tone you wanted it to maintain, falling back into the massive pools of formal, bureaucratic training text it has memorized.

The technical fix: Remind the assistant who it is supposed to be by typing this jargon-pruning directive:

"This sounds a bit too robotic and corporate. Please rewrite this draft using a warm, conversational, and direct tone, as if a kind friend were speaking across a kitchen table. Completely leave out any formal business jargon."

3. The Text Stalls or Cuts Off Mid-Sentence

What it looks like: The AI is typing out a beautiful response, and then it suddenly stops dead in the middle of a paragraph, leaving a sentence completely unfinished.

Why it happens: Every AI platform has a built-in limit on how much text it can generate in a single burst – what the tech world calls a token limit. It simply ran out of operational breath.

The technical fix: The easiest fix of all. Do not retype your prompt or repeat your instructions. Simply type one single word into the box and hit enter:

"Continue"

The assistant will instantly pick up its digital pencil exactly where it dropped it and finish the thought flawlessly.

Reader Reviver Brain Break: The Circuit-Breaker Walkaway

Before we look at the slight differences between the popular AI platforms, let's practice our final somatic reset.

When a computer screen isn't doing exactly what we want, our natural human instinct is to lean forward, pull our shoulders up, glare at the text, and type faster and harder. This physical frustration tightens our chest and completely locks up our flexible, creative thinking.

Let's employ a physical Digital Daisies Circuit-Breaker right now:

The Physical Push: If you are currently facing an unexpected screen or a broken prompt, physically push your chair back away from your desk or table by at least twelve inches.

The Hand Release: Place your hands completely flat on the table, palms down. Feel the cool, stable texture of the wood or surface beneath your palms. Take a deep, slow nose-inhale.

The Stand and Turn: Stand completely upright. Turn your body entirely away from the screen. Walk to the nearest window, or simply take five slow, deliberate steps across the room and back.

The Sixty-Second Clear: Stand still for exactly sixty seconds, letting your arms hang loosely at your sides. Drop your shoulders down away from your ears, and let out a long, sighing mouth-exhale, releasing every ounce of tension.

By physically severing your visual connection to the screen for just one minute, you break the neurological feedback loop of tech frustration.

You drop your stress response, reset your short-term focus, and return to the keyboard feeling completely calm, grounded, and ready to supervise the machine.

Real-World Platform Dashboards

The beautiful language of The Prompt Recipe Method™ is completely universal – it works perfectly across every major tool available today. However, because different technology companies build these tools, the buttons on your screen look slightly different.

Think of it like renting a car: whether you drive a Ford, a Toyota, or a Honda, the gas pedal, the brakes, and the steering wheel all do the exact same things in the exact same way. You just need to glance at the dashboard to see where the buttons are placed.

Let's look at our primary digital dashboards in one clear comparison table:

Feature

ChatGPT (chatgpt.com)

Google Gemini (gemini.google.com)

Microsoft Copilot (copilot.microsoft.com)

The "Whiteboard Clear" (Fresh Start)

Look for a prominent button or sidebar option labeled **"New Chat"** or a simple plus sign (**+**).

Look for a clean option in your menu or sidebar labeled **"New Chat"** or a simple plus sign (**+**) icon.

Look near the primary window or text box for a button labeled **"New Topic"** or a distinct, colorful chat bubble icon.

The Editing Pencil

Move your mouse or tap near a prompt you already sent. A tiny pencil icon will appear, allowing you to rewrite and resubmit your words instantly. Look closely at your sent message block for a small pencil icon labeled **"Edit."** Clicking it lets you adjust your words without retyping the page. Copilot focuses heavily on a continuous conversation stream. If prompt misses, it is usually easiest to type a follow-up correction directly into the new box.

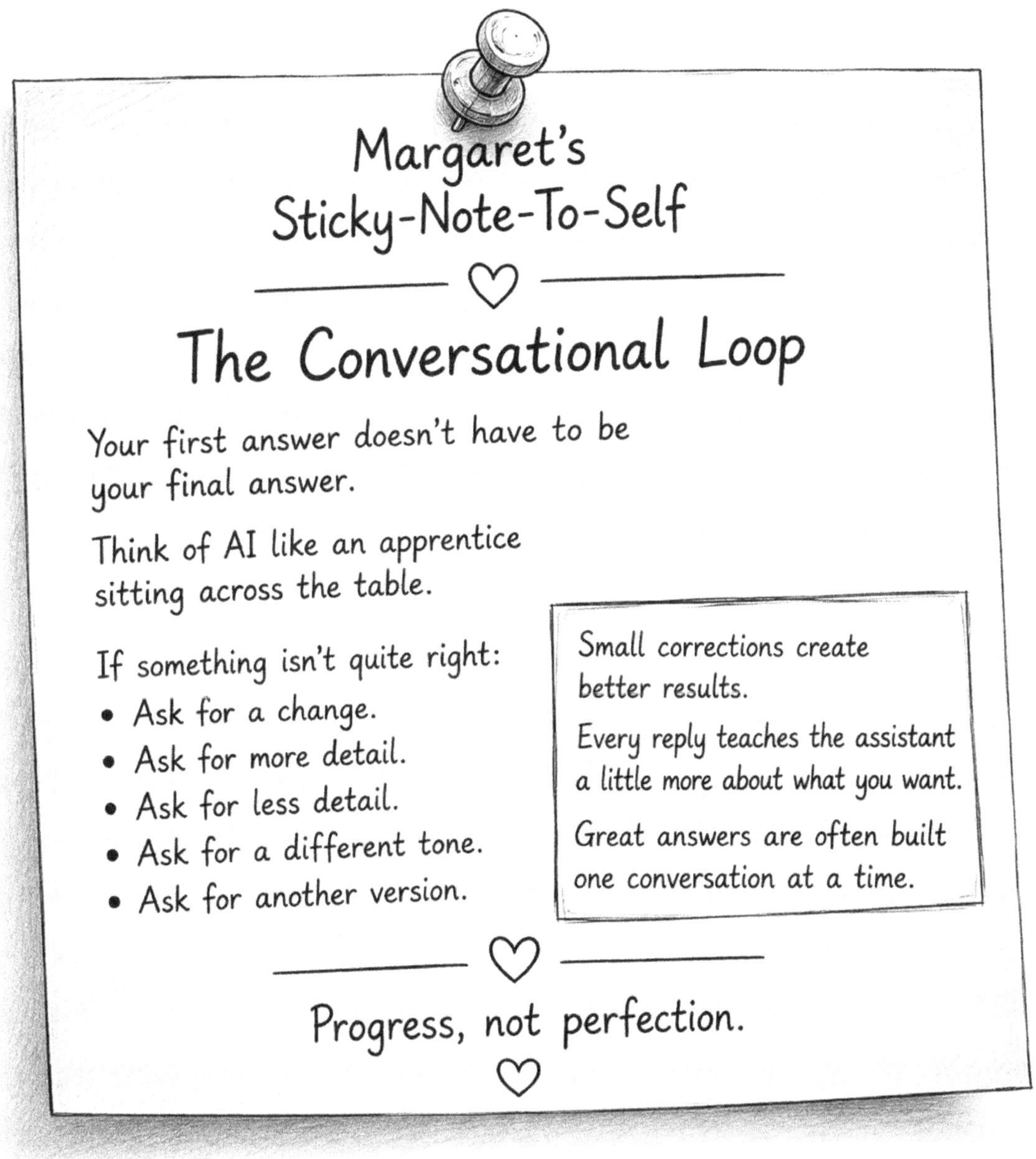

When an output falls flat, remember that you don't have to start over from scratch or come up with a brand-new command. Treat your virtual assistant like an apprentice sitting across from you. If they make a mistake, you don't throw away the whole project; you just say, "That's a good start, but change this one part." You are engaging in a natural conversation. Every correction you enter guides the pattern-matcher closer to your true intent, turning a rough draft into a custom masterpiece through simple, small improvements.

The Recipe in Action: Before and After

To see how these simple troubleshooting phrases instantly salvage a conversation, let's look at a live example of an unhelpful interaction being turned into a high-utility result right in the chat window.

The Missing Recipe (The "Before" Context)

Imagine typing a quick request for a travel list, only to watch the assistant deliver a stiff, clinical response filled with heavy commercial padding and unhelpful bullet points:

“Per standard regional guidelines, travelers occupying transient lodging in the mountain districts must maintain proper apparel criteria. It is imperative to leverage multi-layered garment protection systems to mitigate the effects of variable thermal indices. Furthermore, please find enclosed the required documentation templates...”

The Instantly Steered Correction (The "After" Result)

Instead of getting frustrated or closing the screen, you put on your supervisor hat and type this simple correction right below the robot's answer:

"This sounds a bit too robotic and corporate. Please rewrite this draft using a warm, conversational, and direct tone, as if a kind friend were speaking across a kitchen table. Strip out all that legal padding and give me a plain bulleted list of clothing layers for cold weather."

Instantly, the machine corrects its course and hands you exactly what your eyes need:

Warm Clothing Layers for the Mountains

Base Layer: Lightweight, snug cotton or thermal tops to trap skin warmth.

Middle Layer: A cozy fleece jacket or a thick wool sweater to insulate against the chill.

Outer Layer: A sturdy, windproof winter coat to protect you from unexpected mountain rain or snow.

Look at how easily that was fixed. You didn't break the system, and you didn't have to learn a single line of coding. You simply redirected your intern with plain, everyday English.

The Supervisor's Sovereignty Guide

As you step into permanent digital independence, always remember that you are the primary supervisor standing on solid ground. The machine can analyze language patterns, but it has no heart, no common sense, and no real-world wisdom. If a tool suggests an asset category that looks confusing, or an error fix that feels a bit off, trust your gut and overrule the computer!

You possess absolute authority over the conversation loop. You are not a passive reader following a computer's script; you are an active manager directing a high-powered assistant entirely on your own terms.

Mini-Milestone: Your Permanent Independence Blueprint

Let's pause and note the incredible milestone of digital leadership and independence you have reached right here:

Pattern Gaps: You learned that a vague or robotic AI response is just a simple pattern gap, one you can fix completely within your own power without starting over.

Jargon Pruning: You mastered the specific conversational phrases needed to instantly strip out corporate jargon and robotic language.

The Stalled Text Fix: You discovered the magic of the one-word "Continue" command to instantly restart a stalled text stream.

Somatic Calm: You used a Circuit-Breaker Walkaway Break to maintain complete physical and mental calm when technology acts up.

Dashboard Mastery: You mapped out the dashboard buttons for ChatGPT, Gemini, and Copilot so you can pivot between platforms with total ease.

Take a brief moment to write down your response to this final reflection prompt in your notebook:

Now that I know I cannot break the machine, and that I possess the exact verbal tools to correct any strange response, how does my confidence feel compared to when I first faced the blinking cursor?

The Comprehensive Fixer Cheat Sheet

Use this practical lookup matrix whenever a digital hiccup crosses your screen. You can copy this clean table layout directly onto your desk clipboard:

Situation Encountered

What It Actually Means

Immediate Corrective Action

If Text Stalls Mid-Sentence

The machine hit its internal token limit and ran out of breath.

Type **"Continue"** into the box and press Enter.

If Tone is Stiff or Jargon-Heavy

The assistant dropped its persona and used default training text.

Type **"Rewrite this using a warm, conversational tone and strip out the corporate filler."**

If Output is Boring or Vague

The recipe was missing specific boundaries or local background.

Type **"That's a bit too generic. Add specific real-world context and constraints."**

If the Screen Freezes Completely

The local internet connection flickered for a split second.

Click the circular **"Refresh"** arrow at the top of your browser or close the app.

If Your Mind Feels Fried

Tech frustration is locking up your creative paraspinal muscles.

Employ the **Circuit-Breaker Walkaway**: push back your chair and walk away for 60 seconds.

The Gate is Wide Open

Look back at the remarkable journey you have completed over these chapters.

You started at the very beginning, standing before a blank, blinking cursor with a sense of quiet hesitation and uncertainty. You worried about the jargon, about making irreversible mistakes, or about being left out of the modern digital landscape.

But look at where you stand right now.

You hold a complete, structured mastery over the language of input. You know how to command the most powerful technologies of our era with nothing more than your natural human language, beautifully mixed with your decades of rich life experience, wisdom, and common sense. You are no longer on the outside looking in; you are actively shaping the digital canvas to suit your lifestyle.

You have learned how to use your assistant to clear your inbox, organize your travel and schedules, summarize long-form text blocks, preserve your precious family legacy, nurture your backyard garden pastimes, and ignite fresh waves of personal creativity – all while practicing gentle somatic resets that keep your body relaxed and your mind razor-sharp.

You are not behind. You are not too old. You are an independent, capable creator navigating the modern landscape entirely on your own terms.

The whiteboard is clean, the table is open, and the assistant is waiting. Go ahead and click that "New Chat" button, type your next brilliant recipe, and imagine what becomes possible. Your digital confidence is entirely real and belongs to you. Let's keep creating, one beautiful prompt at a time!

Your Companion Toolkit

Thank you for joining me on this journey.

The following printable resources were created to help you continue building confidence long after you've turned the final page.

Inside you'll find:

✓ A 21-Day Progress Tracker

✓ A Troubleshooting Quick-Fix Matrix

✓ A Personal Prompt Recipe Workbook

Print them, save them, scribble notes all over them, and make them your own.

Remember, confidence doesn't come from memorizing technology.

It comes from using it.

One conversation.

One prompt.

One small success at a time.

Turn the page and let's unpack your toolbox.

GLOSSARY

Definitive Plain English

Welcome to the official, one-stop home for our vocabulary. As promised back in our introduction, every single technical term we use in this book is defined right here, cleanly and clearly, exactly once. You will never have to stumble over these words or wade through dense academic explanations while reading our practical chapters.

Think of this glossary as a quick-reference filing cabinet. If you ever look at a screen and feel a momentary flash of jargon fatigue, simply flip back to this page, grab your plain-English definition, and clear away the confusion instantly.

AI hallucination: A digital quirk where an AI model hits a gap in its pattern library and confidently invents an incorrect date, a false name, or an unrealistic fact rather than admitting it doesn't know the answer. It is not a mistake you made; it is simply a pattern slip that you can easily steer back on track using your troubleshooting toolkit.

Anti-Cliché Valve: A specific wording constraint used in the Prompt Recipe Method™ that explicitly commands the AI assistant to block boring, overused internet tropes, corporate filler, or commercial store-bought answers. By tightening this "valve" in your instructions, you force the machine's pattern-matcher to deliver truly unique, creative, and hands-on ideas .

Artificial Intelligence (AI) chatbot / digital assistant: The conversational computer program or software application (such as ChatGPT, Gemini, or Copilot) built to simulate human-like discussion. It functions like a highly efficient, virtual assistant or a friendly librarian waiting at a desk to process assignments for you.

Bulletin Board Test: A simple visual quality-control check you perform as a supervisor after the AI generates a printable flyer or public announcement. You close your eyes for two seconds, open them, and verify if the absolute main points – the Who, When, and Where – are instantly visible in bold text. If they are buried in long paragraphs, you instruct the assistant to bring them to the top so they don't get lost on a crowded community wall

Context window: The total amount of conversational text, memory, and background information that the AI chatbot can realistically remember or hold onto during a single, continuous discussion session before the screen resets or older messages begin to fade from its active memory.

Cross-Platform Prompt: A prompt, template, or skill that works across more than one AI tool. For example, a prompt that works in ChatGPT may also work in Gemini, Claude, Copilot, or other AI assistants with only minor changes.

Iterative Grounding: The stress-free process of steering or correcting your AI assistant's output by simply typing a normal follow-up note in the chat box without clearing your screen or starting over. Because prompting is a conversational loop, you use your authority as the supervisor to tell your digital intern to shorten a draft, soften a robotic tone, or correct a mistaken detail .

New Chat (Whiteboard Clear): The dashboard interface button or icon (often marked with a plus sign +) that erases your active screen layout and gives your assistant a completely fresh slate. It acts like a physical whiteboard eraser, ensuring background notes from a previous topic don't accidentally spill over into your next prompt task.

Output: The text, answer, or draft that the AI generates and displays on your screen in direct response to the prompt you just sent. This is the final baked cake resulting from your prompt recipe.

Placeholder: An anonymous text bracket, such as [My Bank] or [My Utility Provider], used to temporarily replace private information when drafting prompts. It allows the AI assistant to safely format your writing while keeping your true personal details hidden at home on your own desk.

Platform: A software program, website, or app where you use AI. Examples include ChatGPT, Gemini, Copilot, Claude, and other AI tools.

Prompt: The literal instruction, question, or sentence you type into an AI chat box to tell it what you want. Think of it simply as the custom recipe or assignment you are handing to your virtual assistant.

Prompt Recipe: The core, six-ingredient structural framework used to clarify your text box instructions. It systematically combines a specific Role, Goal, Context, Constraints, Format, and Example to ensure you secure an accurate, custom response on your very first try.

Raw Thought Dump: A low-pressure drafting technique where you type or speak a completely unedited, scattered, or disorganized stream of consciousness into the prompt box without worrying about grammar, punctuation, or chronological order. You simply hand this "messy pile" of facts, frustrations, or memories to your assistant, letting the Prompt Recipe sort it into an elegant, polished layout for you.

Search engine: A traditional internet lookup system (like Google or Bing) that matches short, choppy keywords to pages of online links. Unlike conversational AI tools that answer you directly, search engines require you to manually sift through pages of commercial websites and personal blogs to locate an answer.

Somatic reset / Digital Daisies reset: A brief, 5-minute physical micro-habit or breathing break paired with your computer tasks. These intentional movements calm your physical nervous system, drop subtle tech frustration, and relieve eye or posture strain so you can retain your mental focus.

TL;DR (Too Long; Didn't Read): A common internet abbreviation used to provide a quick summary of a longer piece of text. You will often see a "TL;DR" section at the beginning or end of articles, emails, blog posts, or AI responses.

Token: A basic unit of text (roughly equal to four letters or three-quarters of a single word) that an AI model uses to process and count data under the hood. You don't need to count them yourself; just know that platforms have a built-in token limit on how much text they can generate in a single burst before needing a simple command like "Continue" to keep going.

Web browser: The primary application program you use on your computer, tablet, or mobile phone to open and view internet websites. Common everyday examples include Google Chrome, Apple Safari, and Microsoft Edge.

Value-Added Download Section

Welcome to your digital companion page. If you have been printing out your blueprints, taping scripts to your desk clipboard, or simply want a quick, hands-free way to practice your somatic resets away from these pages, you have arrived at the right window.

Below is the exact text to be placed on the layout page alongside your printable **QR Code** graphic. This text is written in Margaret's signature, warm voice, guiding your readers seamlessly from the printed page onto their devices with absolute peace of mind.

Your Digital Companion: The Somatic Prompt Fixer Toolkit

Pull your chair out for a brief moment, let your hands rest loosely on your lap, and take a long, magnificent breath. You have journeyed through the primary chapters of this book, and your digital confidence is now completely real.

To support your ongoing, independent success, I have gathered all of our time-tested visual organizers, quick-reference tables, and physical resets into one single, easily accessible home off the printed page. Think of this downloadable toolkit as your personal, stress-free roadside safety net – designed to sit right on your device or desk clipboard whenever you need a fast, plain-English reminder of who is in charge.

What is Waiting Inside Your Toolkit:

The Printable Prompt Recipe Matrix: A clean, single-page reference sheet featuring our six core bowls (Role, Goal, Context, Constraints, Format, and Example**) so you can map out custom inputs with total ease.**

The Master Look-Up Cheat Sheet: A laminated-style visual guide of our five emergency course-corrections – including the one-word "Continue" **stall fix – ready to slide right next to your keyboard.**

Somatic Reset Audio Guides: Gentle, A 5-minute Confidence Reset plus four additional 60-second voice tracks guiding you through The 20-20-20 Optic Reset**,** The Scapular Pinch**, and** The Circuit-Breaker Walkaway **so you can release muscle tension completely hands-free.**

Ready-to-Use Copy Blueprints: A digital catalog of all our community flyers, asset tables, legacy scribes, and cancellation letters, allowing you to highlight, copy, and paste placeholders in seconds.

How to Secure Your Download in Under 30 Seconds:

Grab your smartphone or mobile tablet.

Open the built-in Camera app on your device, just as if you were preparing to snap a lovely photograph of a family gathering.

Hold your device steady and point your camera lens directly at the square grid pattern illustrated below. You do not need to click a button or snap a picture; simply let the lens focus on the box.

Tap the small yellow banner or web link that instantly pops up across your screen.

If your device doesn't utilize a camera scanner, you can access your toolkit completely manually by opening your internet browser and typing this exact plain-English address into the long bar at the top of your screen:

"The machine holds the digital pencil, but your life experience and common sense are the true engines fueling the results. Never rush your learning, enjoy the low-pressure experiments, and remember that your digital autonomy belongs entirely to you. Happy creating!"

THE 21-DAY CONFIDENCE BUILDER

A Gentle Roadmap to Real AI Confidence

WEEK 1

FOUNDATIONS & CALM INPUTS

DAYS 1–7

- ☐ Day 1 Chicken/Fish Challenge
- ☐ Day 2 Placeholder Query
- ☐ Day 3 Broad Question
- ☐ Day 4 Custom Role Prompt
- ☐ Day 5 New Chat
- ☐ Day 6 Hobby Search
- ☐ Day 7 Glossary Review

WEEK 2

PRACTICAL CORRESPONDENCE & LISTS

DAYS 8–14

- ☐ Day 8 Appointment Email
- ☐ Day 9 Text Editing
- ☐ Day 10 Graceful Decline
- ☐ Day 11 Packing List
- ☐ Day 12 Road Trip Table
- ☐ Day 13 Recipe Menu
- ☐ Day 14 Document Grid

WEEK 3

CREATIVE SPARK & INDEPENDENCE

DAYS 15–21

- ☐ Day 15 News Summary
- ☐ Day 16 TL;DR Practice
- ☐ Day 17 Book Club Themes
- ☐ Day 18 Gift Ideas
- ☐ Day 19 Journaling Prompts
- ☐ Day 20 Continue Command
- ☐ Day 21 Platform Switching

THE SOMATIC COMPANION TRACKER

21 GENTLE PAIRINGS FOR A CALMER, CLEARER YOU

- ☐ 1 Optic Break
- ☐ 2 Security Exhale
- ☐ 3 What Surprised Me
- ☐ 4 Posture Check
- ☐ 5 Grounded Feet
- ☐ 6 Shoulder Blade Drop
- ☐ 7 Deep Stomach Breath
- ☐ 8 Scapular Release
- ☐ 9 Open Chest Posture
- ☐ 10 Jaw Relaxation
- ☐ 11 Finger-Tap Rhythm
- ☐ 12 Wrist Stretch
- ☐ 13 Visual Break
- ☐ 14 Breath Pause
- ☐ 15 Eye Tracking
- ☐ 16 Mind Reset
- ☐ 17 Seated Torso Twist
- ☐ 18 Horizon View
- ☐ 19 Hand Extension
- ☐ 20 Circuit Break
- ☐ 21 Total Calm

MARGARET'S STICKY-NOTE-TO-SELF

Confidence doesn't arrive all at once. It grows one calm conversation at a time.

PROGRESS, NOT PERFECTION. SMALL STEPS. BIG CONFIDENCE.

THE DOUBLE-SIDED TROUBLESHOOTING MATRIX

Quick Fixes for You and Your AI Partner

Great conversations sometimes hit tiny snags.
Use this matrix to reset, refocus, and keep moving forward.

WHEN THE ISSUE IS... YOU

Check in. Reset. Choose one small action.

WHAT YOU MIGHT FEEL	TRY THIS
Overwhelmed →	Take a slow breath. Simplify one step.
Stuck or confused →	Step away. Come back with fresh eyes.
Low energy or motivation →	Stand up, stretch, or do a 2-minute reset.
Unsure what to ask →	Start simple. Use a placeholder question.
Worried about making mistakes →	Remember: This is practice, not a test. You're learning!
Frustrated or losing patience →	Pause. Exhale. Kindness helps both of you.

WHEN THE ISSUE IS... YOUR AI

Adjust your input. Guide with clarity.

WHAT YOU MIGHT SEE	TRY THIS
Confusing or off-topic response →	Clarify your question. Add more context or restate simply.
Too vague or generic →	Ask for specifics. Use examples or a clear format.
Missing key information →	Add the missing details. Try: "What else would you need?"
Repeats the same idea →	Shift your angle. Ask it to try a different approach.
Too long or complex →	Ask for a summary, bullets, or a simpler explanation.
Doesn't follow instructions →	Break it down. Use numbered steps or clearer rules.

THE RESET ROUTINE (WORKS FOR BOTH SIDES!)

1. PAUSE – Stop. Take a breath. →
2. CHECK – What's not working? →
3. ADJUST – Make one small change. →
4. TRY AGAIN – Keep it simple and clear. →
5. CELEBRATE – Progress counts. Always.

REMEMBER

You and your AI are a team.
Clarity + patience + practice =
better answers, better results,
and growing confidence.

Margaret's Sticky-Note-to-Self

Every snag is a setup for a stronger skill.
Stay kind, stay curious, and keep going!

SMALL ADJUSTMENTS TODAY. BIG CONFIDENCE TOMORROW.

MY FAVORITE PROMPT RECIPE

The simple formula I'll use again and again. ♡

MY FAVORITE PROMPT RECIPE FOR: ______________________ ♡

[ROLE] Who should AI be?
Act as a: ______________________
____

[GOAL] What do I want?
My main goal is to: ______________________
____

[CONTEXT] Helpful background details.
The background details are: ______________________
____
____

[CONSTRAINTS] Boundaries and rules.
Please follow these strict rules: ______________________
____
____

[FORMAT] How should the answer be arranged?
Arrange the final answer as a: ______________________
____

THE BEST SOMATIC RESET TO PAIR WITH THIS TASK IS:
____
____

Margaret's Sticky-Note-to-Self ♡

♡ A clear prompt + a calm body = better answers, less stress, and more time for what matters. ♡

♡ SAVE IT. USE IT. REFINE IT. REPEAT. ♡

MY FAVORITE PROMPT RECIPE

The simple formula I'll use again and again. ♡

MY FAVORITE PROMPT RECIPE FOR: Planning a Weekly Meal Plan ♡

[ROLE]
Who should AI be?

Act as a: a friendly nutritionist and meal planning expert

[GOAL]
What do I want?

My main goal is to: create a healthy, balanced 7-day meal plan that is easy to prepare and fits my busy schedule.

[CONTEXT]
Helpful background details.

The background details are: I'm cooking for one. I prefer simple recipes with common ingredients. I'd like a mix of vegetarian and lean protein options. I have about 30 minutes each evening.

[CONSTRAINTS]
Boundaries and rules.

Please follow these strict rules: Keep recipes under 500 calories per serving. Use affordable ingredients. No highly processed foods. Keep prep time under 15 minutes when possible.

[FORMAT]
How should the answer be arranged?

Arrange the final answer as a: table with columns for Day, Breakfast, Lunch, Dinner, and a short recipe idea. Include a grocery list at the end.

THE BEST SOMATIC RESET TO PAIR WITH THIS TASK IS:

Two-Minute Reset: Stand up, roll my shoulders, take three deep belly breaths, and smile.

Margaret's Sticky-Note-to-Self ♡

♡ This is just one great example. Make it your own, save it, and let it save you time again and again. ♡

♡ ONE GREAT PROMPT TODAY. EASIER DAYS AHEAD. ♡

MY FAVORITE PROMPT RECIPE

The simple formula I'll use again and again. ♡

MY FAVORITE PROMPT RECIPE FOR: ______________________

[ROLE]
Who should AI be?

Act as a: ______________________

____

[GOAL]
What do I want?

My main goal is to: ______________________

____

[CONTEXT]
Helpful background details.

The background details are: ______________________

____

____

[CONSTRAINTS]
Boundaries and rules.

Please follow these strict rules: ______________________

____

____

[FORMAT]
How should the answer be arranged?

Arrange the final answer as a: ______________________

____

THE BEST SOMATIC RESET TO PAIR WITH THIS TASK IS:

____

____

Margaret's Sticky-Note-to-Self ♡

♡ A clear prompt + a calm body
= better answers, less stress,
and more time for what matters.
♡

♡ SAVE IT. USE IT. REFINE IT. REPEAT. ♡

One Last Little Favor?

*****Review*****

You did it!

You've made it all the way through AI Prompts for Absolute Beginners Over Fifty, and that is something worth celebrating.

Not long ago, the idea of writing prompts for artificial intelligence might have sounded confusing, intimidating, or something best left to younger generations. But here you are – learning how to ask better questions, get better answers, and use AI as a practical tool in everyday life.

More importantly, you've discovered that you don't need to be a technology expert to make AI work for you.

Whether you're using prompts to write emails, organize your day, plan a holiday, brainstorm ideas, learn something new, or simply make life a little easier, you've taken a powerful step forward.

Now, if this book helped you, I would be incredibly grateful if you would consider leaving a short review on Amazon.

Your review might be exactly what another beginner needs to see before deciding to give AI a try.

Think of it as leaving a friendly note on the café table for the next person who walks through the door.

By leaving a review, you're helping to:

• Encourage other beginners to take their first step with AI

• Build confidence in people who think technology has passed them by

• Support the creation of more easy-to-follow books for learners over fifty

• Grow a welcoming community of curious minds who are learning together

Thank you for allowing me to be part of your journey.

The world of AI is changing quickly, but one thing never changes: learning becomes easier when we help one another.

And if you've made it this far, you're no longer just reading about AI.

You're using it.

Please leave your review on the platform where you found this book, or use this link:

[https://www.amazon.com/review/review-your-purchases/?asin=BOOKASIN]

With gratitude, encouragement, and a warm cup of coffee,

Margaret Fields
Digital Daisies & Curious Bytes
A Tech Series for Bold Minds Over Fifty

From the Author

Before we part ways, I'd like you to take a moment and reflect on how far you've come.

When you first opened this book, you may have felt curious, cautious, excited, overwhelmed – or perhaps a little bit of all four at once. New technology has a way of making even capable, intelligent people question themselves. It can sometimes feel as though the world is racing ahead while we're still trying to find the right button to press.

But look at where you are now.

You have learned how to communicate with AI using clear prompts. You have explored practical ways to use these tools in everyday life. You have discovered that getting useful results is not about being "good with technology." It is about learning a few simple patterns and having the confidence to experiment.

Most importantly, I hope you've discovered something else along the way.

You do not need to know everything. You do not need to memorize every feature. You do not need to keep up with every new announcement, update, or trend... You simply need enough confidence to stay curious.

The people who thrive with new technology are rarely the people who know the most. They are often the people who are willing to ask questions, try things, make mistakes, and keep learning one small step at a time.

That is exactly what you've done throughout these pages.

If there is one idea I hope you carry forward from this book, let it be this:

You are not behind.

You are learning at your own pace, in your own way, and that is more than enough.

The digital world does not belong only to younger generations, technical experts, or people with engineering degrees. It belongs to anyone willing to explore it with an open mind and a little patience.

Including you.

So keep asking questions.

Keep experimenting.

Keep pressing the occasional wrong button and discovering that the world does not end.

And whenever technology feels confusing again, remember that confidence is not something you have before you begin.

Confidence is something you build by continuing.

Thank you for spending this time with me. Sharing this journey has been a genuine pleasure, and I hope this book has helped make technology feel a little less intimidating, a little more useful, and perhaps even a little more enjoyable.

Put the kettle on, give yourself credit for what you've learned, and when you're ready, keep exploring.

I'll be cheering you on from the next book, and every new adventure that follows.

Warmly,

Margaret Fields

www.ingramcontent.com/pod-product-compliance
Lightning Source LLC
LaVergne TN
LVHW060038210926
848481LV00013B/3892